I Am Maria

I Am Maria

My Reflections and Poems
on Heartbreak,
Healing, and
Finding Your Way Home

———

MARIA SHRIVER

THE OPEN FIELD · PENGUIN LIFE

VIKING
An imprint of Penguin Random House LLC
1745 Broadway, New York, NY 10019
penguinrandomhouse.com

The Open Field/A Penguin Life Book

THE OPEN FIELD is a registered trademark of MOS Enterprises, Inc.

Designed by Amanda Dewey

LIBRARY OF CONGRESS CATALOGING-IN-PUBLICATION DATA
Names: Shriver, Maria, author.
Title: I am Maria: my reflections and poems on heartbreak, healing,
and finding your way home / Maria Shriver.
Description: New York: The Open Field, 2025. |
Identifiers: LCCN 2024058177 (print) | LCCN 2024058178 (ebook) |
ISBN 9780593653395 (hardcover) | ISBN 9780593653401 (ebook)
Subjects: LCGFT: Poetry.
Classification: LCC PS3619.H7747 I25 2025 (print) |
LCC PS3619.H7747 (ebook) | DDC 811/.6—dc23/eng/20241209
LC record available at https://lccn.loc.gov/2024058177
LC ebook record available at https://lccn.loc.gov/2024058178

Printed in the United States of America
1   3   5   7   9   10   8   6   4   2

The authorized representative in the EU for product safety and
compliance is Penguin Random House Ireland, Morrison Chambers,
32 Nassau Street, Dublin D02 YH68, Ireland,
https://eu-contact.penguin.ie.

—————

I started trying to write some version of this book
more than twenty years ago
I'd start then stop then start again
I always ended up putting it down
I wasn't ready
I finally am

On a hilltop in Petaluma, California
I buried the woman who wrote much of what's on these pages
The woman who was tougher than tough
I buried the part of me that was filled with
Self-loathing self-criticism self-hatred and self-judgment
I buried the combative angry controlling version of myself

On that hilltop I asked for forgiveness from God
For the pain I caused myself
For the pain I caused others
And for the pain they caused me
That process was extremely emotional and deeply revealing
It was liberating
It has given me a new beginning

I never imagined I would write a book of poetry
I never imagined writing poetry would help me embark
On a journey deep into myself
I never imagined that everything I sought or thought I needed
Was within me all along

What I found in writing poetry is that
You never know where it will lead you
But if you remain open
It just might lead you to your own Open Field

The poetry within these pages comes from
The front lines of my life
I've learned that many of the things I write about in these pages
Are felt by millions of other people
Which is what led me to finally think publishing them
was a good idea

This is a book about love and longing
Loss and liberation
Heartache healing and hope
It's about finding the light and love within and all around

It's about being in communion with all the different parts of oneself
It's how we mend our hearts and souls
It's how we find our way home

Ultimately, it's about surrender and salvation
Because I've learned that while our paths vary
We are all on a quest of our own
Your quest can help guide mine
And mine can perhaps help guide yours

My hope is that while reading these poems
You will feel there is healing and freedom on the other side
Of the trauma, the pain, the regret, the judgment
You may have experienced or may be experiencing
Freedom from the self you think is you
Freedom from that harsh dark voice that lives inside
of so many of us

We all need compassion for ourselves and love for ourselves
We all need to forgive ourselves and accept ourselves
For once all this is given
Healing can arise

Climbing the mountain that is me has been excruciating,
grueling, and deeply emotional
But also freeing
It was a climb that only I could do
It's not something one can outsource
And you can do the same if you so choose
There is no doubt in my mind about that

This book is dedicated to all those
Who are brave enough to make that climb
And it's dedicated to my beloved children, grandchildren,
And my entire family
It's also dedicated to all those who loved me
And tried to love me along the way
You know who you are
I see you and I love you
I really do with my whole heart and soul
Until the end of God's time

Love always,
Maria

———

Out beyond ideas of wrongdoing and rightdoing,
there is a field.
I'll meet you there.

—Rumi, thirteenth-century
Persian poet and mystic

———————

Out beyond wrongdoing and rightdoing
Out beyond fear, expectation, and judgment
Out beyond shame, pain, and grief
There's an Open Field.
I'll meet you there.

—Maria, 2025

My Reflections and Poems

Reflections

I am Maria.

Believe it or not, it's taken me a lifetime to be able to say that and feel it was enough. That may be somewhat surprising, but stick with me here, and I'll try to explain.

Searching for the authentic Maria—uncovering, discovering, and recovering her—has been a challenge for me all my life. For decades I couldn't see her, because I was looking for myself in all the wrong places.

Of course, I didn't know it, because I thought I had the self-awareness thing down cold. In fact, in 2000 I published the bestseller *Ten Things I Wish I'd Known Before I Went Out into the Real World* because I wanted to share all the lessons I'd learned about love, marriage, kids, and how to navigate your way into a high-powered career—everything I thought you needed to know if you wanted to "have it all" in this life, as I thought I did.

I was forty-five years old at the time, and I ended the book with

"I'll get back to you in ten years." That's when I just knew I'd be ready to publish a self-congratulatory update on how extraordinarily well I'd done by continuing to apply those same ten lessons to my own life. In fact, I was sure I'd be able to come up with ten more pithy bits of hard-earned wisdom about love, marriage, kids, and career by then.

But when I did turn fifty-five years old, I was in no emotional shape to write a book. In fact, I was barely able to get out of bed. So much for my delusions of self-awareness.

Well, now I'm into my sixties, and thank God, I'm up and out of bed, standing on my own two feet. Getting here hasn't been easy, but I'm grateful to have finally learned some real hard truths about life and about myself that just might be worth passing on.

You may be wondering what on earth took me so long to see these truths? Trust me, I've asked myself that question a million times. But I now understand that I couldn't have known these truths until I learned them—and I couldn't have learned them until I lived them—and I couldn't have lived them until I had to.

I had to when circumstances forced me to break through my lifelong, industrial-strength wall of capital-D Denial, so I could come face-to-face with the self I had left behind—the self I had buried under a pile of relationships, accomplishments, titles, and false beliefs. No one did that to me. I did it to myself.

So under all of the rubble, I had to ask "Who was Maria?" The beginning of getting some real answers came when I started writing poetry.

I'VE ALWAYS LOVED POETRY. Years ago, I discovered Mary Oliver's poem "The Journey," and it spoke directly to my soul. When I turned fifty, a friend gave me a copy of Derek Walcott's poem "Love After Love," and I felt like it was written for me and about me. And then I discovered the poet and mystic Rumi, who talked about that field "out beyond wrongdoing and rightdoing." Over the years, I'd even taken a stab at writing poetry myself, but I always seemed to just skim the surface of what I was feeling inside.

But now all of a sudden and to my surprise—in the darkest period of my life—when I sat down and put pen to paper, all the stories I'd been telling myself, all the walls I had built up around myself, started to fall away, and what I was actually feeling poured out of me in the form of poems.

WHEN MANY PEOPLE think of poetry, they think of rhyming couplets or Shakespearean sonnets. I did, too, and that made the idea of writing poetry intimidating to me. But once I gave myself the permission to just write down whatever I was feeling—words that were true, that were raw, that made me feel vulnerable, that didn't even have to make sense—I found that poetry was the way for me to express what was buried deep inside. All of a sudden poetry didn't feel out of reach to me anymore. It didn't have to rhyme, it didn't have to fit into a certain structure, it didn't have to have narrative cohesion. It just had to be true. So true, it often shocked me.

As someone who's written several books and countless speeches and essays over the years, I thought I had already uncovered much of what I wanted or needed to say about my life. But when I discovered poetry, I found a new voice inside me. I felt my heart cracked wide open and my soul was set free.

Since then, I haven't stopped writing poetry. It has given me a path to freedom that I've never felt before, and it is how I've been able to address most directly and authentically the truth of my own past and present reality—and my hopes for the future.

I'VE RIPPED MANY of these poems out of a place of fear, shame, confusion, and darkness—a place I'd buried deep within me decades ago. Writing them often made me feel ashamed—and I would cry and shake as I read them back, stunned at what had come out of me.

Eventually I embraced the fact that through my poetry I was able to give voice for the first time to my lifelong anxiety; my lack of self-worth; my persistent feeling of emptiness, longing, and loneliness—and that giving voice to all that was a good thing. And it's turned out that revealing my reality to myself—the fragmentation, the isolation, the anger, and the fear—hasn't been as painful as hiding all of it from myself for all those years.

YOU SEE, I grew up in a big, competitive Irish Catholic family, where you didn't sit around and talk about your feelings. You went out into the world and had an impact. The bar was set high, and I mean *really* high. When I looked around my family, I saw that if you weren't *doing*—if you weren't serving, if you weren't striving, if you weren't accomplishing and accomplishing *BIG*—then you weren't even seen. You really didn't even exist.

In our family, achievement brought visibility, recognition, and acceptance. That's the way my family lived their lives, and I saw them changing the world and being acknowledged and honored, even revered, for it. So naturally a child surrounded by all that would believe that overachievement was not only expected of her, but would give her worth, self-worth, and visibility within the family and out in the world. And even more important, overachievement out in the world would bring what every child craves more than anything: love. This child believed that was the secret to getting her mother's love and attention.

In fact, one of my earliest and happiest memories of connection with my mother was on the campaign trail with her.

IT's 1960, and I'm almost five years old. We live in Chicago, and we're standing outside in the freezing cold in front of a great big office building. As people rush in and out of the revolving door, my mother is stopping them, handing them leaflets, introducing herself, and asking them to vote for her brother, John F. Kennedy, for president. I mimic her—stopping people, giving them leaflets, asking them to vote for my uncle Jack. I really don't understand exactly what it is we're doing, but I know my mother is in her zone—changing minds, getting votes, helping her brother achieve his dream. I like it too—even though I'm freezing my ass off—because I can feel that I'm making my mother proud. I feel useful, I feel good, and I feel loved.

MY UNCLE JACK's subsequent victory brings a whirlwind of change into my young life. In what seems like a minute, my family is packing up and moving from Chicago to Washington, DC. My parents hit the ground running and never look back.

My mother immediately starts pressuring her brother to create a President's Panel on Mental Retardation, which he does. It's my mother's favorite cause, in honor of their intellectually disabled sister, Rosemary. At the same time, my mother is also turning our home and our big backyard into a summer camp for hundreds of children with intellectual disabilities and dedicated volunteers—a camp that will eventually grow into the International Special Olympics movement. And my father? He throws himself into scouring the country for "the best and the brightest" to serve in Uncle Jack's cabinet. He then goes on to start the Peace Corps, the War on Poverty, Head Start, Job Corps, Legal Services for the Poor, and so many other programs that changed our country and the world.

OUR NEW HOME becomes a home base for people who believe they, too, can change the world for the better. On any given weekend, the home I share with my parents and brothers—plus twenty dogs, horses, pigs, chickens, a monkey, and a snake—is exploding with Kennedy administration officials, priests, nuns, doctors, scientists, social workers, businessmen—all of them mixing and mingling with wide-eyed Peace Corps volunteers, idealists from around the country, and people with intellectual disabilities from Camp Shriver. It's chaos, and everyone loves it.

I WANTED TO LOVE IT, too, and I often did. But the crazy, nonstop world my parents created also felt overwhelming to me, at times. The busy-ness swirled all around me, and I often felt alone in the middle of it—a feeling exacerbated by being the only girl in a family with four brothers.

To escape the chaos, I would often head off by myself to the stables to find peace and companionship with my pony. Being with her helped calm me, gave me a place to be myself and to be by myself. Sometimes I'd even sleep in the stables to find a space of my own away from the whirlwind swirling around what was the Family Business: people, politics, purpose, and service.

. . .

BUT MAKING ROOM for myself to think, dream, or simply be just wasn't something my parents understood. They were people of action. That's what they respected, and it's what they expected. They ran a house where you weren't allowed to sit down for even one second, otherwise you'd hear, "What are you doing sitting down? Get up, get out, and do something to help others!" My parents wanted us to live out the dictum my grandmother had drilled into all of us: *"From those to whom much is given, much is expected."* At home, I heard that over and over again.

And when I went out into the world, it felt like there were even more expectations to fulfill. Everywhere we went, people greeted us with squeals of excitement and appreciation—their reaction to the Kennedy accomplishments, glamour, wealth, fame, and great teeth and hair.

> *"Hey, aren't you a Kennedy? Which Kennedy are you?"*
> I would say, "I'm Maria."
> *"No, no, no! You're Caroline, right?"*
> "No, I'm Maria. I'm Maria."
> *"Aren't you Bobby's kid?"*
> "No . . ."
> *"Wait! You must belong to Teddy then!"*
> "No, I'm Maria! I'm Maria Shriver."
> *"But you're a Kennedy, aren't you?"*
> "Yes, but I'm *Eunice*'s daughter."

Disappointment would cloud their faces. Then they'd brighten: *"But Eunice is a Kennedy, isn't she? So you're a Kennedy, right?*

*Right? Can we get a picture with you? Can we touch you? We love
the Kennedys! We wanna say we met a Kennedy!"*

Enough experiences like that, and the message was burned into
my little brain: *Maria isn't enough. Being Eunice's daughter isn't
enough. Being a Shriver sure isn't enough. Being Maria Shriver for
double sure just isn't enough.* Fighting that message and changing
that narrative became my lifetime motivation and goal.

So as young as I was, I made a pact with myself. I promised myself
that this child who felt invisible both within her huge, high-profile
family and out in the world would work her butt off to become so
successful that people would stop asking her which Kennedy she
was. They'd stop being disappointed when they learned who she
wasn't. I promised myself that people would just plain know *me*:

"Hey! There's Maria! That's Maria Shriver!"

I figured when people finally knew me, *I* would know me. I
promised myself I'd get so very good at something—anything!—
that even my parents would have to stop and take notice of me. And
in that promise to myself, my grit and determination were forged.

So first I came up with Plan A: I'll become a champion horseback
rider! Great idea, I thought. I loved horses, I loved riding, I loved
competing, and I especially loved the power and the freedom I felt
when I rode, so I dove right in. Eventually, I got so good, I started
winning ribbons and championships and thought, "Hey, maybe I'll
go all the way to the Olympics!" But then I discovered boys, and
whoops! The horse shows fell off my radar.

Okay, on to Plan B: I'll become a supermodel! People had always told me I was pretty, so I thought I'd go for it. I daydreamed about having my name and face on magazine covers all over the world. I practiced modeling bathing suits and demonstrating beauty products in front of the bathroom mirror. But then I discovered Dunkin' Donuts and pizza, and that one went out the window too.

Undeterred, I went on to Plan C: I'll become the first nun in the family! Yes! I was at an all-girls convent school, and I saw how much respect the nuns got from everyone—especially my parents, who seemed to idolize nuns and priests. Yup, that's it! I'll become Mother Maria, and I'll start schools and missions. That's how I'll help people and change the world!

But then I saw *The Sound of Music*, where I heard the Reverend Mother tell the young nun who ironically shared my name, "*Maria, these walls were not meant to shut out problems. You have to face them. You have to live the life you were born to live.*" I remember sitting in the movie theater feeling like she was speaking directly to me, warning me I wasn't cut out for the convent. And then when I learned that nuns took vows of poverty and chastity, that sealed it for me. I raced home, ran into my bedroom, slammed the door shut, threw myself on my knees, and prayed, "Dear God, please, *please* don't call me to become a nun!" (And by the way, apparently the nun thing didn't look so good to the Maria in the movie either, because she left the convent and married an Austrian. Hmmm . . .)

THE TRUTH IS, what really dashed my girlhood plans and dreams were the life-shattering events that happened out in the real world:

the assassinations of my uncle Jack when I was just eight years old and then my uncle Bobby when I was twelve years old.

In the wake of these public tragedies, the outside world stopped cold in its tracks, but no one in my family seemed to stop for one minute. No one stopped to cry, no one stopped to talk, to grieve, no one stopped to offer comfort, certainly not to me or my brothers. For me, it was confusing, even terrifying. I could feel that these events rocked the world and ruptured my entire family's life, especially my mother's—but she never spoke about them to me or anyone else. Neither did my father. They both dug in and carried on.

I learned how to cope with trauma, loss, sadness, and grief by doing what everyone in my family seemed to do: annihilate the feelings by pretending they didn't exist, shoving them down by working more and harder—not collapsing, not talking about the pain, not giving up, and most important, not giving in. What I heard was, "There are so many other people out in the world worse off than you! Buck up, act strong, put a smile on your face, get back out there, and be an example. I don't want to hear another yip out of you, not now, not ever!" And they didn't.

So even in those times of trauma, when I felt so unsafe, the mantra was still, *"From those to whom much is given, much is expected."*

MY PARENTS DID all they could to make that mantra come to life. They wanted me to be self-sufficient, tough, and grateful. They didn't want me or my brothers to be spoiled. They wanted us to understand our privilege, to recognize that those without resources, very often without hope, lived very different lives from ours. And they felt it was important for us to personally experience how others lived and do all we could to make a difference.

To that end, they sent me to live and work with people very different from myself. I lived in a hogan on a Navajo reservation in Arizona. I lived with a family in Bethel, Alaska, in the dead of winter. When I was fifteen, they sent me to West Africa to live with a family in Tunisia, where I worked with children. The following year they sent me back to Africa to work alongside Peace Corps volunteers in Senegal. I know their hope was that, like them, I would find a passion for a life in service.

Well, the truth is I didn't find passion for service on the reservation or in the snow or the streets of Tunis or the fields of Senegal. But in all those places, my grit, my determination, my independence, and my individuality did take root and grow. And it all made me realize that if I didn't figure out what I wanted to do with my life, my parents were more than willing and capable of figuring it out for me. And if they did, they'd send me off to the Peace Corps, or sign me up as a Special Olympics director, or even worse, run me for office. Needless to say, I was determined none of that was going to happen to me.

THANK GOD THAT IN 1972, Plan D revealed itself. That's when presidential candidate George McGovern chose my father, Sargent Shriver, as his vice presidential running mate. At the time, I was still living in Senegal. Out of the blue, I was told to pack my bags and come home immediately and get to work on the campaign.

Before I knew it, I was flying all over the country with my dad as he went from campaign stop to campaign stop. On the campaign plane, when there were no seats left in the front with him and his team, I was relegated to the back. And that's when my life changed forever.

Because that's when I discovered that the real action wasn't in the front of the plane where my family sat, analyzing and strategizing with their campaign advisers. No. To me, it felt like the real action was in the back of the plane, where the journalists were—working and talking and laughing and competing with one another. All day long, the reporters asked questions and got answers. Watching and listening to them was exciting and made me feel alive. What they were doing appealed to my natural curiosity, my interest in how others lived and worked, and my desire to make a difference.

"This is it!" I thought. "I don't belong in the front with my family. I belong in the back of the plane with these people!" The reporters from newspapers, wire services, and the radio and TV networks were the only ones on the plane who actually seemed to be having fun. And not only that, they had what I thought was the more important and interesting job: telling the world what the politicians were thinking, saying, and doing. To me, the reporters were the ones who were framing the debate, crafting the story, telling the country what was really going on. To me, there seemed to be more power and influence in the back of the plane than in the front. *Bingo!* I was hooked.

I thought to myself, "This is how I'm going to get away from my family and politics and still be in the much-is-expected-of-me game! I'll be a television journalist! No one in my family does that. I'll become my own person, do my own thing, build my own identity, have my own life, achieve my own accomplishments. And I'll still be able to make my grandmother and parents proud, because I'll go out and find and tell the stories of invisible people in need. My work will shine a light on the problems they face and hopefully uncover solutions."

Finally, I had a real plan! What a relief!

Well, the McGovern-Shriver ticket went on to lose the election and lose big—and my father's crushing defeat made this seventeen-year-old furious. The idea that Richard Nixon was considered a winner and my father a loser pissed me off. The Family Business of politics disgusted and enraged me. The unfairness of it, the hypocrisy of it. To me, politics now meant assassinations, chaos, loss, grief, and humiliation, and I hated it. It all made me more convinced than ever to pursue my own personal trajectory, to get as far away from politics as I could get.

So when I was twenty-one and had just graduated from George-town University, I started applying for jobs at local television stations. And then two months later, something beyond my wildest dreams happened to me. I met my very own Austrian—and my world shifted seismically.

THIRTY-YEAR-OLD Arnold Schwarzenegger looked and sounded different from anyone I'd ever met before—and his career in championship bodybuilding was as far away from politics and my family as I could ever get.

My attraction to him was instantaneous. He was brash, funny, charismatic, and most intriguing and appealing to me, it felt like he was a free spirit. He wasn't burdened by others' expectations or demands. In other words, for me he represented freedom from everything I wanted to run away from and everything I wanted to run toward.

IN MANY OTHER WAYS, he also felt familiar. I felt at home around his relentless drive, his competitive energy, his larger-than-life personality. He wasn't threatening or scary to me. He felt a lot like people in my own family. Like me, Arnold was also in the Big Expectations business. He was someone I could share my dreams with, and he wasn't intimidated by them, because his were as big if not bigger than mine. He told me "I want you to go for it, and I won't stop you—because I want to go for it, too, and I don't want anyone to stop *me*." Now that might not sound romantic to you, but to me, it was a turn-on.

So off we went. We started dating while each of us pursued our individual dreams—his to become a big movie star, mine to become a big network morning news anchor. Neither of us ever doubted the other's dreams, and our individual work ethics helped fuel each other's ambitions.

FIRST, I got myself a local television news job in Philadelphia, and I moved there. I knew people at the station were skeptical about "the Kennedy Kid" who showed up in the newsroom, so I knew I had to prove myself. I started working my way up from the bottom by working my butt off. I took whatever they threw at me and ran with it. I worked the overnight assignment desk. I monitored the police scanner. I made coffee for everyone. I didn't break when the news director screamed at me in front of the newsroom. I kept my head down and continued to work and work and work.

In time, I got promoted to the day shift. I went out with reporters to help them on their stories. I logged their tapes in the edit room. Then I moved to a station in Baltimore. I worked behind the scenes some more. Then I got a job as a soundwoman on a camera crew out in the field. From there I worked my way up to be a producer. I worked and worked and worked in the trenches. All of it made me even more determined than I was already.

Then after a couple of years, I made what was for me a really big personal decision. I decided to leave behind everything and everyone I knew on the East Coast and move to the West Coast to be with Arnold full time. I told my mother it was temporary, but in my heart I knew it wasn't.

My family was shocked and worried. You see, no one understood my relationship with Arnold. They all thought it was just a rebellious phase I was going through and that I would for sure grow out of it. After all, Arnold was a Republican, a bodybuilder, and someone who said he wanted to be a movie star. He lived in a two-bedroom apartment and wore a Speedo. He was as far away from Washington and Hyannisport as I could get. They thought I couldn't possibly be serious. But I knew differently. I had always felt I would need someone different from what I had grown up with. As the only daughter in a family with four brothers and dozens of male cousins, I knew it would take a strong man to deal with all the testosterone swirling around in my family. And I knew it would take someone who was independent and confident to deal with me.

I was driven, relentless, independent, hyperfocused—in fact, very much like my mother. She was, in many ways, my role model. In Arnold, I felt I had not only found my match, but also found a partner who'd keep me safe—safe from the world, safe even from the demands and pressures of my family—someone with whom I could build a different kind of life, my own life. Our life.

While I was aware that not everyone saw in Arnold what I saw in him, I was in love with him and went with my gut. I was fiercely protective of my decision to be with him. I was determined to prove myself right and prove the naysayers—those who didn't believe in me, him, or us—wrong.

IN LOS ANGELES, I gained a sense of freedom I didn't have on the East Coast. I was happy. And with time, I made another decision: to get out from behind the camera and take a shot at being in front of the camera.

I was told I had to lose weight (lots of it), go to a voice coach to learn how to sound like an anchorwoman, and dye my hair blonde. I did two out of three. I got a local TV news job and threw myself into it. As time went on, I continued moving up, eventually getting to the network, assigned to stories all over the country and the world.

Then, in the year I turned twenty-nine, two big things happened one after the other. I got engaged in July and then in August, I finally got offered my dream job: anchoring a network morning news show. At last! My dream come true! Even though we had just gotten engaged, Arnold encouraged me to take the job. It meant living in New York during the week, getting up every day at 3:00 a.m. to get to the studio, and then commuting home to LA on the weekend. No problem! I wore big shoulder pads, had big hair, and did big interviews. Then the following spring, Arnold and I got married. I was in heaven—running, running, running a million miles an hour.

And then, BAM! Out of the blue, the show got canceled and we all got fired. I was heartbroken. But I was determined to bounce back. So I changed networks, got a new job, and got back to work. Then I got pregnant. When I had morning sickness, I smiled on-camera—"I'm Maria Shriver. Back to you."—then puked in the bucket next to me on the set during the commercials. The stage-hands laughed.

FINALLY, I was Maria Shriver! I had my own separate identity from my family's. It was built on my own track record, which earned me Emmys and the coveted Peabody Award. I wrote my own bestselling books. I had my own life, my own career, and my own family, which eventually included four children. And even though I was a member of one of the most prominent Democratic families in the country, I had even married a Republican and survived!

But ironically, without realizing it, I was busy re-creating the chaos of my youth. Like my parents, my husband and I were on a fast track. And just like my mother, I was racing round at a hundred miles an hour, and nothing could stop me—not a cousin's fatal drug overdose, not another cousin's fatal ski accident, or a third cousin's deadly plane crash. Not my husband's emergency heart surgery, not my mother's failing health.

FAST-FORWARD TO 2003 and *kapow!* My movie-star husband abruptly decided he wanted to run for governor of California. Wait, *WHAT?* You gotta be kidding me! I told him I didn't want him to do it. The mere thought of him running brought up tremendous trauma for me. I was so scared he would be assassinated like others in my family had been. If not that, I was terrified he would lose like others in my family had. And I was also terrified that if he won, my kids and I would lose him forever to politics and the public, just as I had lost others in my family.

For decades, I had worked tirelessly to help him achieve his dreams. But this dream felt more like a nightmare to me.

As I TRIED to stop him, my mother intervened. She said, "Don't do that. Listen to me: He'll never forgive you if you dash his dreams. Be a team player, and go out there and support him, regardless of what you want." I knew in my heart she was right.

I took a deep breath, and just as I had done with his movie career, I threw myself into helping him make his next big dream a reality. I put my upbringing to work. I hired people to help him. I stood in for him at campaign events. I stood up for him when his character came under attack. I worked my ass off for him. And after a surreal and lightning-fast campaign with more twists and turns and cliffhangers than any of his action movies, he won.

Once again, politics upended my life. Overnight, scores of new people—staff, handlers, hangers-on—poured into our home. I was back in the Family Business again—but this time with Republicans! It was surreal. And then before I knew what hit me, my network news bosses called to ask me for my resignation, because they said my having a politician for a husband gave the appearance of a conflict of interest—and *poof!*—my hard-won career of twenty-five years in journalism evaporated.

THERE'S A SAYING that if you don't deal with your demons, they'll come back and bite you in the ass. Well, bite me they did. All of a sudden, everywhere I went, people shouted, "*Hey, aren't you the*

Governor's wife? Aren't you Arnold's wife? Where's Arnold?" I was now "the Kennedy married to Arnold Schwarzenegger."

Here I was, living a life of privilege, power, and fame—filled with all the excitement, glamour, visibility, and high drama so many people dream of—and once again, when I stood still, I felt exactly like I did when I was a kid—invisible and alone, disconnected, disoriented, and empty, and it scared me to death. And right then came a real moment of truth, when I realized deep in my soul that all my solutions—the external fixes, the nonstop work, the toughness and determination that had motivated me for so long—hadn't made me feel secure and good enough about myself deep down in my core. The fact was, it felt like nothing had changed since I was a kid, and I was shocked.

OBVIOUSLY IT DIDN'T shock me enough, because did I do something different? Nope. Instead, I tried to ignore the feeling, immediately pivoting to what I had learned so many years earlier: dissociating from and numbing any pain or questions or dissatisfaction I had by throwing myself into work and the achievements I felt were expected of me and that I expected of myself.

IN AN EFFORT to cope with it all, I did what I always did. I came up with a new plan and a new promise to myself: I'll become an amazing First Lady of California! I'll work my way into it. I'll be the perfect political partner. I'll work hard. I'll be well dressed. I'll smile. I'll be bipartisan. I'll give speeches. I'll champion women, the working poor, and families dealing with Alzheimer's. I'll save the California History Museum. I'll write several more books. I'll run an enormous, high-energy, high-profile California Women's

Conference, attracting the biggest names on the planet, and everyone will attend or want to attend. I'll even travel all the way to India to convince the Dalai Lama to come speak, and he will. I'll make my husband and my family proud.

Oh, and I'll be home every night for dinner to make sure my four kids feel happy, loved, and secure, even though they, too, have been thrown overnight into a situation where they're being guarded twenty-four hours a day by the California Highway Patrol.

LET ME STOP here to say that I'm so very grateful I got to serve as First Lady of California, and I'm proud of the job I did. Performing that kind of public service turned out to be a huge blessing for me. As First Lady, I found community with women all over the state. I met people who became lifelong friends. I found new ways to express myself and new ways to make a difference. I have to admit that the role I didn't want turned out to be the best job I ever had. It combined my upbringing, my knowledge of politics, my curiosity and creativity, and my journalism all into one job. It helped me find my own voice, it gave me new freedom and new confidence, and it helped me forge new pathways into the future for myself.

That said, there were times during this period that I felt lonely and lost. I felt like I needed to be everything to everyone, and like no matter where I was, I was always in the wrong place. I shuttled myself back and forth between Sacramento and Los Angeles, and anytime I was in one city, I felt like I needed to rush to get back to the other.

And then there were my ailing parents back east. My father had just been diagnosed with Alzheimer's, and my mother was slowly going downhill, breaking hips and having strokes. More often than not, I felt like I should be traveling across the country to care for them too. It was a lot.

The truth is that throughout my life, I was always worried about my mother's health. She had come close to death several times, but she always defied the odds and bounced back, because she was tough as nails and refused to give up. That's just who she was. She was a towering figure not only to me, her only daughter, but to my father, my four brothers, and everyone in our extended family. My mother was relentless, passionate about her work, smart as hell, the one with all the answers.

In fact, she was the dominant figure in my life, the person I spoke to several times a day every day. She was my biggest cheerleader, my anchor, the person who pushed and prodded me, the one I most wanted to please and make proud. I loved her deeply, admired her tremendously, and wanted to emulate her in so many ways.

But now, just when I felt like I needed her the most, I was losing the ability to talk things through with her, to ask her advice, to get her perspective. Strokes were robbing her of her strength and her voice. But even as I saw her getting sicker and sicker—and as I shuttled back and forth between LA and her hospital rooms in various cities on the East Coast—it was inconceivable to me that she wouldn't bounce back yet again.

Well, one thing you learn in this life is that believing you're in control is just an illusion. When your time is up, it doesn't matter who you are or who you know. It's just up.

IT WAS THE BEGINNING OF August when I got a call like so many I'd gotten over the years. It was one of my brothers saying, "I'm taking

Mummy to the emergency room." I got on a plane, like I'd done so many times before. But this time would be different.

Sitting in the hospital ICU—something I'd done countless times—it began to dawn on me that what I'd feared most in my life might actually be happening now. As I sat staring down at my mother, I thought about her life. I thought about all the pain she had endured, the loss she had suffered. I thought about all the grief she had carried in her life, and I thought about how tough she'd had to be, so she wouldn't break. I thought about how hard she had worked at her roles of daughter, sister, wife, mother. I thought about how tired she must be. My heart went out to this towering figure of a woman, who had worked relentlessly to make a difference. I knew she had tried to change the world for those with intellectual disabilities—and had done so. But I also felt that deep down, she had also been trying to be noticed within her own family, where all the accolades and credit had always been focused on the men. There is no doubt in my mind that she had driven herself that hard because she was trying to prove to her parents and her brothers that she mattered, that she was enough, and that she was as good, as tough, and as accomplished as any man in her family. My heart broke for her, even as I realized that my own struggles mirrored hers.

I remember leaning in and taking my mother's frail hand and squeezing it tight. Normally, she would have pulled it away, because she wasn't into physical affection. But this time was different. She let me hold her hand. It reminded me of the time she let me climb into bed with her a few months before when, for the first time in my life, she let me hold her and talk to her about how much I loved her.

Now she couldn't speak, but she did open her eyes, and I know she heard me, and I said, "Mummy, you did such a great job with your life. I'm so proud of you. I love you so much. I'm so grateful you are my mother." I told her my brothers and I were all doing fine, that we all loved one another deeply, and that we would all stay close. I told her how proud I was to be her only daughter. I assured her I was going to be okay without her—even though I didn't believe that for one second. I told her that her job here was done, and she was now free to go.

Twenty-four hours later, with all her children and grandchildren around her, she died.

As I EXPECTED, her death knocked me off my feet. I was overcome with grief to the point where I was sure I wouldn't survive. Then two weeks after she passed away, my uncle Teddy, the patriarch of our extended family and her best friend, also died.

Then a year and a half later, all hell seemed to break loose. My First Lady job came to an end. My father died two weeks later. And then came another devastating, life-altering blow: my twenty-five-year-long marriage blew up. It broke my heart, it broke my spirit, it broke what was left of me.

Without my marriage, without my parents, without a job—and with two of my kids already moved away to college and a third on his way out the door—the dam of my lifelong capital-D Denial just blew apart. I can only describe it as sitting alone in the ruins after a tornado whips through.

Now, much has been written about the end of my marriage, and frankly I don't feel like I need or want to discuss it here, or anywhere for that matter. I've made a very conscious decision not to engage in that conversation in the public square or anywhere else, because I don't think doing so helps anyone, especially my children. In my view, the end of one's marriage—even if it happens between two public people—is extremely private and should stay that way. I've made a deliberate decision to keep my own counsel, respect everyone's privacy, and while it hasn't been easy, it's been what is right for me.

THAT SAID, I do want to take a moment to acknowledge the grace, valor, and courage my children exhibited during that time and every day since then. Everything about their world and the sanctity of their home got uprooted in an instant. They managed this extremely painful public and private situation with class and elegance. They had to learn how to silence the public noise so that they could do the deep work of healing themselves. They had to find the strength to ignore other people's insensitive opinions about a situation no one could have even fathomed, much less understood. They had to forge their own path to forgiveness. They had to do the hard work of reestablishing their relationships with both of us individually and as their parents, just as Arnold and I have done with each other.

IT TAKES TREMENDOUS inner fortitude to hold one's own inner counsel and not react to every comment thrown your way. It takes tremendous work to heal one's heart and reestablish a sense of safety within oneself and one's new home. My children Katherine, Christina, Patrick, and Christopher are four extraordinary human beings who did all of this and more, and I couldn't be prouder of them. Their work has been nothing short of heroic. They continue to work at building their own lives in their own way and in their own time. Everyone involved continues to work on finding their way forward and creating a new version of our family.

As for me, the feelings I felt at the end of my marriage are hard to put into words. I was consumed with grief and wracked with confusion, anger, fear, sadness, and anxiety. I felt emotionally bereft and disconnected from life as I knew it. I also felt deeply disconnected from myself—or who I thought I was. I had been with Arnold since I was twenty-one years old—my entire adult life. I barely remembered who I was before I met him. I was unsure now of who I was, where I belonged, or who I belonged to. Honestly, it was brutal, and I was terrified.

I knew I was in uncharted territory and that I had serious work to do if I wanted to survive. I also knew that while the end of my relationship with Arnold was heartbreaking, it wasn't the sole source of the heartache I carried. No single person or relationship can claim that title. Over time I've come to learn that a full life distributes heartbreak across many different moments, loves, and losses— each unique in its own way. It's up to us to find healing or, at the very least, to make sense of it all ourselves. I knew what was ahead of me was going to be hard—really, really hard. It was going to be scary and uncertain. Somewhere deep down, though, I knew I could survive. I knew that I *had* to survive. As I sat on my hotel room floor in the dark, terrified and alone with tears streaming down my face, I thought to myself: Maria, this doesn't have to be the end of you. It *can't* be the end of you. Make it a new beginning of you.

. . .

IN THOSE ENDLESS DAYS, I asked myself a thousand questions, the most important ones being: *Who is Maria anyway? How the hell did she end up here?*, and *Who is she now?* I realized I'd lost track of the answers a long time ago. All of a sudden I saw with great clarity that I'd been running around like a lunatic since childhood, searching for myself in all the wrong places. All those years, when I looked in the mirror and believed I saw myself clearly, it turns out I was wrong—because I was looking at myself through my family's eyes, through my bosses' eyes, through my husband's eyes, through the public's eyes.

Now I didn't know who the hell I was looking at. I had spent a lifetime running away from the authentic me, and I had succeeded. Now when I looked in the mirror, I had to acknowledge that the woman staring back at me was someone I had built from the outside in, layer upon layer. I didn't know that woman, and I had lost respect for her. Sure, I didn't like it when people identified me by the role I was filling—a Kennedy, a TV anchor, the governor's wife—but that's what I did to myself as well. Now I was waking up and asking, "Who am I apart from all that?"

I WON'T BORE and exhaust you, as I did my friends back then, with the details of my self-pity party. I admit I had one, and it lasted a long time. I'm also going to spare you a litany of all my trips to various therapists, healers, shamans, mediums, and psychics. I won't tell you how many self-help books I read, how much money I spent on candles and crystals. I started a meditation practice. I did yoga, Pilates, and plant medicine—everything I could think of to get stronger and better.

Thank God so many old friends and new friends checked in on me repeatedly. They listened to me go round and round in my own head. They spoke to me calmly, assuring me that I was okay and that I would be okay, and they reminded me over and over that I was the woman they loved, the woman they believed in, a woman they knew would triumph. It was a master class in friendship, and I was the beneficiary.

IN MY SEARCH FOR ANSWERS, help, and guidance, I even went across the country to a cloistered convent. Yes, I did do that, because I'd always felt drawn to the peace and community of the convent. At the end of my stay there, Mother Dolores gently took me aside, and in what once again felt like a scene right out of *The Sound of Music*, she said to me, "Maria. I understand that you like it here very much, and I can tell you feel at peace here. But if you're thinking you can come live with us, let me tell you, you can't. Our cut-off age is fifty, and you're fifty-five!"

And then she went on to say exactly what I needed to hear. She looked me straight in the eye and said, "I think what you're really looking for, my child, is permission—permission to leave your marriage, permission to go forward, permission to live, permission to be Maria." She continued, "I have spoken to our Mother Superior, and she told me I could give you that permission. Now go out there, my child, and become Maria." She hugged me, and then we both wept.

BECOME MARIA? WAIT! WHAT? How do I become Maria now, when all the titles and trappings are gone? Who is Maria without all of that? This wise nun was telling me it was up to me to figure it out. It was up to me to wade through the muck and the mess, question my beliefs, push past my history, my decisions, my mistakes, and go out and build my own life. And for the first time, I realized I'd have to build my life from the inside out. Oh, my God! How do I do that? Where do I even begin? I had no clue.

I BEGAN BY MAKING A conscious decision to do everything differently than I'd done before. I decided to slow my life down, so I could feel and hear myself. I decided not to throw myself back into the sixteen-hour workdays that had always been my comfort zone—and believe me, I know I'm very fortunate to have the wherewithal to slow down my work schedule. I turned down practically everything that came my way—television work, speeches, appearances, books. I put my focus on my kids and myself and slowly found a new work rhythm that worked better for us.

I must admit there were times when ego made me want to hit the fast-forward button again—like the big payday dangled in front of me with an offer to have my own daily talk show. But I used my shaky voice to say *no*. I was determined to stick with my promise to try to do everything differently.

And now when I made myself sit still, I could feel what I had avoided my whole life: enormous emotional pain and grief. Actually feeling it was horrible, and I recognized that much of it was old. I realized I had spent my life batting away and disavowing any pain that came up, because I was terrified of it, and I never felt entitled to it. Who was I to complain? Who was I to cry "Ow!" when something hurt? *"Get a grip! There are so many other people in the world worse off than you!"* I had internalized that message and made it my own. I had been tough on me, but now all that tough self-talk only made me feel worse and ashamed.

So I read. I read Emerson's "Self-Reliance." I read and reread Anne Morrow Lindbergh's *The Gift from the Sea.* I read "Solitude of Self" by Elizabeth Cady Stanton. I read *Revolution from Within* by Gloria Steinem. I read *When Things Fall Apart* by Pema Chödrön. I read Dorothy Day, Melody Beattie, Anne Lamott, Martha Beck, Sister Joan Chittister, Thomas Merton, Father Richard Rohr, as well as poets like Mary Oliver, John O'Donohue, Rumi, and Hafiz. Philosophers, self-help gurus, priests, feminists, monks and nuns and saints. And I went to therapy, all kinds of therapy.

But all the therapy and reading and inner-child work and candle burning and talking and praying and intellectualizing got me only so far. I knew if I wanted to change and grow, I needed to go further and deeper. I would have to be brave enough to take off the layers of armor I'd been piling on since I was a child. Now I knew that armor was shielding me not only from danger, but from myself.

I HAD ALWAYS been a writer, writing news stories and articles and gratitude journals and books. But now I started writing from a deep place within, and the kind of writing I was doing—deliberate, uncompromising, truthful—was poetry. Yes, poetry! And lo and behold, this stream-of-consciousness poetry helped crack open my armor and get at what was underneath. My words flowed out of me with a renewed purpose. For the first time in my life, I allowed what came up to come up—without judgment. And the more that came up, the deeper I went. Through my poetry, I've found, and am still finding, a woman who was terrified of not being able to live up to her family's legacy—scared of not being big enough, scared of not being good enough, a good-enough daughter, a good-enough sister, a good-enough wife, a good-enough mother, a good-enough journalist. A good-enough human being. I've also discovered, to my surprise, a woman who is tender, sensitive, vulnerable, kind, creative, and spiritual.

I found a woman who had insisted on measuring herself by some impossible standard that guaranteed she'd come up short and feel bad about herself no matter what. I found someone who had spent a lifetime avoiding grief over the death and the loss of not only people she loved, but of her own self. And I also learned that when that lifetime of dissociated grief and trauma is released, it rushes out like a tsunami, and it feels like you're going under and can't breathe. But there also came a shocking and critical lesson: that I am strong enough to survive my own grief, my own pain, my own loneliness.

WITH TIME AND A LOT of work, I've had to confront and then rip up the list of what I thought were my beliefs, but were actually theirs or his or yours. Beliefs about success, beliefs about power, beliefs about Catholicism, beliefs about marriage and divorce, beliefs about right and wrong, beliefs about courage and bravery. For instance, I was raised to see bravery through a very narrow lens. For me, bravery always involved being competitive—like winning the race down the black-diamond ski run or winning a race for public office. I was raised to believe bravery meant never giving up, always hanging in no matter what.

Wrong. My poetry has shown me a new definition of bravery. I've learned it's brave to be emotionally honest and vulnerable. It's brave to be open, especially after you've been hurt. It's brave to stand up for yourself. It's brave to change your mind when you realize you were wrong. It's brave to choose yourself over someone else, especially when that means moving into unknown and uncharted territory. It's brave to admit your mistakes and ask for forgiveness—and then it's really brave to move forward, particularly when you're terrified. And it's brave to choose love over everything else, especially love for yourself.

LIKE EVERYONE, I've made lots of mistakes. One of them was tying my self-worth to my achievements out in the world. Another—and this is a biggie—was thinking I had to work to earn love. It took me a long time to learn that you don't have to achieve anything in order to be worthy of love. You just are. Another big mistake was thinking that someone outside of me could guarantee my safety, my security, my worth, and my peace.

With time, I've also had to come face-to-face with other misguided beliefs—about aging, about being dependent and *in*dependent, and about being alone. I used to believe that if you didn't have a partner, you must be unworthy and unlovable. I've learned that nothing could be further from the truth. Just because I'm alone at the moment I'm writing this, that doesn't mean I'm not lovable. It doesn't mean I'm not whole. I know there are people who assume that because I'm not with someone right now, I couldn't possibly be complete and happy. But the truth is I am. I have so much love in my life. I feel whole. I've come to see myself and be proud of myself as a survivor. I've survived my history, and I've survived how I regarded myself and how I treated myself for all those years.

My poetry has helped me uncover all of this, feel it, see it, express it, and accept it. And it has given me peace and acceptance.

AT FIRST, I didn't want anyone to read my poems, as they are deeply personal, and I worried they would not measure up to the classic definition of what poetry is. But eventually, I showed some of them to a few close friends, and they urged me to share them, because my poems ignited their own self-discovery. My hope is they may do the same for you. I hope you will write your own poetry to find yourself, too, to uncover in your past what your mind has worked very hard to cover up, to reconcile your hopes, dreams, and expectations with the reality you are living today. If you have been journaling for years, or keeping a diary, and are feeling less inspired by that practice, I encourage you to try poetry to go deeper into your thoughts and feelings. Poetry is incredibly powerful and can help you tap into your unconscious, where so many insights are hidden. I believe anyone can do it and feel its power in their own life, as I have in my own.

AT THIS POINT I want to say that this book is not a confessional or a memoir. (I think I'm way too young for that!) On the pages that follow, I share insights into many things I've experienced, but these poems aren't meant to be about any one person or thing. You won't find any salacious and secret-spilling, revenge-spewing *Gotcha!* stories in here. These poems are *my* doing and *un*-doing and *re*-doing. They represent a range of emotions I've experienced over my lifetime and the many lessons incurred over a lifetime as a daughter, a mother, a sister, a wife, and a woman. My daughter calls them

"Reporter Poetry"—raw, authentic reporting of life as it unfolds or through the rearview mirror. Rather than revealing the stories or meaning behind my poems, I prefer for them to stand on their own and stay open to your interpretation.

I KNOW THIS is not your typical poetry collection. This is more of a journey in poetry. And this journey doesn't have a destination. I'm not suddenly healed or enlightened or happy all the time because of the poetry I have written. I don't have all the answers, and I still often struggle to truly be at peace with myself. But I understand life better today. I understand that happiness can come and go. A good day can include both tears and laughter, pain and joy.

What I hope you will find here are poems that chronicle my journey from confusion to clarity, from brokenness to wholeness. They are in the order they appeared in my life. Each poem is a step forward in my life. The universal emotions of loss, grief, joy, awe, wonder, and love are all in these poems, and I hope you can relate to them.

I grew up in the family that I did, and we lived the way we did. That's forever part of me, and I'm grateful to have made peace with it. I fell in love with and married the man I did, and for a long time, we had a great ride. We have four incredible children, and now we're grandparents, and thank God we are friends. Broadcast journalism was great for me. Working for local TV stations and big television networks fueled me, toughened me, made me a storyteller, a writer, and showed me I could excel in a big job, play with the best, and survive the ups and downs that come with a crazy business like that one.

. . .

I'VE WORKED HARD to create and re-create the woman who is me. Like many daughters, I'm different from my mother, but similar in so many ways—both of us restless, driven, smart, funny, family focused, relying deeply on our faith. But I've been able to pursue my vulnerability and my femininity in ways my mother never could. I've been able to find self-love in a way my mother never could. I've been able to slow down in ways my mother never could. And I've been able to find an inner peace my mother never could. That said, my mother is and always will be my greatest role model.

SO NOW THIS WOMAN who has seen so much and felt so little—who has lived big, yet felt small—is standing on the brink of a new era for herself. I'm thrilled that at my age, I actually feel like that! Today on a good day, I feel confident, centered, and strong, thanks to my faith, my family, and my friends. I feel like I'm finally living my own authentic and deeply meaningful life. I know now that there aren't any professional accomplishments that will bring me comfort, joy, or peace. Those feelings can only come from how I choose to walk in my life and who I choose to have walk alongside me. To that end, I'm grateful to so many who have loved me along the way and also to those who tried to love me, but I pushed away. I'm grateful to all the people who encouraged me on my path of self-discovery. They refused to believe my best days were behind me, and they loved me forward until the moment I became brave enough to begin loving myself. Letting go and letting love in has been incredibly healing for me. It's what has finally brought me peace. It has allowed me to embrace all the many parts that make up Maria.

I've learned that no matter how fast you run, life will catch up with you—and when it does, you have to decide if you're going to push it away or pay attention, stop, and reboot. Poetry has been my way of rebooting.

THESE POEMS AREN'T JUST for me or about me though. I'm not interested in revealing everything they mean to me, because it's my hope that they will reveal their own meaning to you. I hope you see parts of yourself in them and that they encourage you to go deep and interrogate your own deepest feelings and beliefs. I hope these poems will help you look at your life with a new clarity, appreciation, respect, forgiveness, and compassion—even wonder—for your own journey. I hope they'll help you get beyond other people's expectations and judgments of you. I hope they'll help you see that we all have within us darkness and light, shadows and clarity—that we all have within us everything we need to survive—that we all can navigate the emotional switchbacks in our lives. I hope you'll see that you don't have to disavow those parts of yourself that may have scared or embarrassed you. Embrace them all. I believe our life's work is to do the deep work of uncovering and understanding all parts of oneself, because all parts of you have value.

There's not good or bad. There's just humanity.

Welcome to the Open Field. Welcome home.

Uncovering

Start Where You Are

Every journey begins where you are
Where you are on your path

Are you afraid?
Are you ashamed?
Are you strong enough to admit you are broken?
Or do you still believe you are whole?
Perhaps you aren't ready for the journey of your life

Dig into yourself
Pause
And pause again
Breathe
Then begin again

Start where you are
Just start
You are ready for the journey that lies ahead.

That Little Girl

See that little girl
Why does she run so
What makes her so frantic
So frenetic
So wild
What do children run from?
Is it their fears
Is it their lives
Is it their truth

Children are as children are
One day you will meet that child in you
And she will smack you like a wave
Look at me she'll say
I am your freedom
I am your truth
You have left me
You have left me to be
Be what
Be who

Stop now
Stop running from me
I'm not here to tame your wildness
You have tried all sorts of things
Now try what you've never tried

Be with me
Look at me
Rest with me
Sit
Be
I am you
Look at me

The Child Within

I close my eyes and try to listen to her
To you
I'm scared she says
I need help she says
Over and over she pleads with me
Then I hear the adult
You don't need help
You're fine

No no the little girl says again
I need help
I feel my eyes well with tears as she says help me help me
    help me
I'm alone
I'm afraid

What are you afraid of says the voice of the adult
Full of judgment and scorn
I realize that's my mother talking to me
I know she can't abide fear or weakness
She can't handle neediness
She can't comfort the child in me

Don't come in my room says my mother stay out of
    my room
Get out go away
So I do
. . .

That's my mother's voice
Stern scary terrifying
The child in me is anxious and scared
I wonder about the child in her
Is that child anxious and scared
Nobody saw her
Nobody sees me

The Padded Door

The padded door
It stood guard
Separating her from me
I can see it now so many years later
There actually were two
Two doors that blocked my way
Two doors with padded leather and studs and locks
Two doors that kept out the noise
Two doors that kept me from you

I often knocked but knew you couldn't hear
I often banged but knew I would be met with silence
Once I saw my brother curled up on the floor outside your
    padded door
He was crying
He just lay there whimpering
No one heard him
I watched and listened
I looked and turned away
I didn't pick him up
I didn't hold him or calm him
I didn't know what to do to stop his tears
Because no one stopped mine

I'm sorry I didn't pick him up and take him to bed
I'm sorry I didn't knock down those doors
I'm sorry for the pain that kept you inside that room
Inside your heart

Inside your mind
Padded doors lock out so much
They locked me away from you

The padded door I still see it
I'm still knocking
Can you hear me
Will you ever

In the Morning

As a child I was terrified of the night
The darkness the quiet
Our house was old so I could hear every creak and noise
We lived in the middle of nowhere
Across from a mental institution
I was always sure that if someone bad came
Or something bad happened
No one would ever hear my screams or my cries

My mother lived at the end of the hall behind two double-
    padded doors
When I knocked there was never a response
I knew not to knock
But I often did anyway
Hoping one time she might hear me hear my fears
She never did
I would go back to my room
At the end of the hall
Telling myself
Try again in the morning
The morning would be my chance to shine
In the morning my mother would surely see me talk to me
    comfort me
I always held out hope for the morning

Today I know my morning is never coming
Today I grieve that my mother could never open her door
I grieve that she could never hold me comfort me sit
    with me

I needed that kind of mother love
The kind that comforts eases your pain sits with you talks to you
    Whenever you are scared

Today I know I will never be held or rocked in my mother's arms
Never seen for who I truly am
Never
There is no tomorrow morning
Only the night

Surrender said God
I give up I give in
I say Thy will be done

Small

I feel so small
I always have
So small
In a house where everything was so big
So small that I got lost
Did you notice I was small?
Did you notice I couldn't reach?
Did you notice I was scared?
No of course you didn't
Your door was shut
Your eyes were closed
Your heart
I couldn't find it
Couldn't touch it
Couldn't reach it
It too was lost
Deeply buried in some dark place
I couldn't reach it

I tried all different ways to grow big
Big was what you noticed
Big was what you liked
Big was what I tried to be
I grew up
I grew out
I tried on big
But it never fit
Big was an illusion

Big enough was unattainable
I was too small to be big enough
There were so many bigs in my house
So I left

I found another place to try on big
But I was small there too
I couldn't reach the lights
I couldn't touch what I wanted to touch
And so I gave up

———

I made peace with being small
I gave up trying to be big
I decided it hurt too much
I changed my mind about big
And when I did
I found your big heart in that small little room you hid in
My big heart loves your small little self
I wish you had known how big you already were

You Got This?

Hello
Can you hear me
Is anyone inside
Inside your crazy mind
Your anxious body
Your dark messy room
Hello
Can't you see what's going on out here
There is chaos all around
People getting shot falling down
There is carnage there is violence there is fear all around
You keep talking as if he's living
Don't you see that he is not
Hello
Do you have this or do you not

Hello
Can you protect us from this fear that's raging now
Don't you hear the cries
The longing of your kids
I'm talking to you woman
I've got brothers
I've got children
I'm doing all I can
Is anyone really listening
Is anyone home
Doesn't anyone see what's happening right here
We are dying in this home

. . .

C'mon now
Wake up
Don't you see what I see
We are still here
Still alive
Still breathing
We are crying out for you
We are asking for your help
Say something pleads the child
Speak up
Do you have us
Do you got this
Tell me if you do
If you don't I'll get help
I'll try to save you

I'll get a man
I'll get supplies
I'll get us help
Get up
C'mon now
Please try just this once
Please tell me
Do you have this or do you not

Is There a Man in This House

Is anyone home
Is anyone here to protect me
Protect us
I wonder
But really I know
I think not

I stand at the top of the stairs
The doors are all closed
The floors creak the wind howls
I'm frozen terrified
I cannot move
I dare not move
There is no one here to protect me
I know this instinctively

I look to my right
My father's door is closed
I feel he is incapable of protecting
He never stands up
Never speaks back
Never steps forward
I look down the hall
I know not to knock
Nothing would happen if I did
I know no one would hear me even were I to scream to cry
    to yell
Everyone lives behind closed doors

I stand here frozen in the darkness terrified
My brothers can't help
They aren't yet men

As the sun begins to break through
I return to my room down the hall
I shut my door
Daylight is coming
One more night is over
I made it through
Again

Danger

All around you there is danger
You can feel it
You can see it
You can sense it
Yes you can
Danger
Lurking behind every door
You can feel it
In your body
Deep down in your core
Danger
You're on the lookout
On the alert
Everywhere you go
Every person is a threat
Every situation raises fear
There's danger all around you
It's so very clear
You hold your breath
Your eyes dart here and there
There's danger in our midst
And it's coming so near
Get out get help
Scream or shout

The danger is inching closer
You can feel it yes you can
Your breathing gets shallow

Your anxiety keeps you on guard
The danger comes closer
Your heart starts pounding
The footsteps sound closer and clear
The danger is beside you
In your room in full view
Don't scream don't shout
Just lie there until
Until you have a plan
Until you know for sure
The danger is inside
Your home your bed in you
Get out get free it's all you can do
Take everyone to safety
You can you will you do

My Father

My father who art in heaven
Hallowed be your name
I haven't seen you since you checked out of the game
Are you finally at home
Are you at peace or do you struggle
Are you restless
Are you smiling
Or are you all alone

Do you feel your power more than you did here on earth
Do you continue to follow or dare stand your ground
Are you stable
Are you strong
Do you say what you think
Or silence your voice so you don't a make a stink

Stand up my father
Stand firm in yourself
Tell the world what you think
Do it
Do it for once
Do it for all
Do it for God
Or don't do it at all

Were you happy were you sad
Was pleasing your currency your worth
Was it worth it

Was it worth it
Please tell me what you think

Did you sell your dreams
Did you silence your hopes
Who are you my father
Who art in heaven
Hallowed be thy name
I forgive you your trespasses
As you forgive mine
As we forgive those who trespass against us

Thy will was never done
Thy kingdom never built
But maybe it will be in heaven.

I See You Now

You loved grass and trees
Bushes and bees
Your eyes twinkled with delight at the mere sight
Not just of her but it seemed
Anyone who reached out to talk to you
Dapper delight jacket in place shoes shined bright
Up you got when she walked by
You always said you were the luckiest guy
The luckiest guy
Yes that's what you said
In work and in play
That was your way
You never complained
You prayed you drank you read you put gas in the tank
You had your way
Your way of walking in the world
Your way of holding your ground
Your way of loving her
Your way of standing down

You see all I wanted was for you to stand up
To rage against it all
But now I see that wasn't your way
You had a way of doing things
A way I didn't understand
I wanted you
To speak your mind
To yell out loud

I wanted you to take charge
But you had different plans
You had your own way

I wish you told me your thinking
I wish I'd known your plan
I see now your strength was there
It just was hidden from my eyes
I see you now but I didn't way back when
When the birds swirled the horses ran the dogs barked I ran
I ran away from
The man you were
Now I see what I couldn't have then
A quiet strength a deep resolve a love that conquered all

In Communion with You

You were the first to look into my eyes
the first to connect to my soul
even though there were no words
I knew you understood

Every time I saw your face
my heart skipped a beat
my breathing slowed
I didn't really know
But I felt
I felt in communion with you

Isn't that wild isn't that true
That I was in communion with you
What does that mean what does that say
No words come to mind
I just knew
That time spent with you was what brought me calm
Brought me peace

I remember the day I came looking for you and you were gone
Just like that you had vanished I didn't know why
I searched big I searched low
I desperately wanted to know
So my mother said you went away
Away? queried the girl
To where? she pressed on
She is dead said the mother

Nothing left to do or say
Life just happens that way

I walked to the stables empty now of your smell
The pain was so guttural it felt like sheer hell
I'd been through so much but this was worse than it all
My best friend my confidante
I lay down curled up in a ball and cried like a child

I felt ashamed that the pain was over a horse
But no one understood, of course
The role that you played the hole that you filled
I was in communion with you
And it's never been like that again

Dallas

That word pulls the trigger
Rips through my house like the wind
I can't catch my breath
Or save anyone who's here
Alone in my room
I'm scared

Dallas
Why did you forsake us
Why did you let that happen
Why did you
Where were you

For years I hated you
Sure it was your fault
You changed everything
And then there was nothing
Everything was a shell of what was
The door was locked I couldn't bang my way through
No one could no one did

Dallas
You just stood there with blood on your hands
Blood all over your face
I said one day I'll go to you
Yell at the air
At the building
At anyone who was there

Years passed
The pain didn't

One day I just walked in
Into the door and up the elevator
And out I looked
At the hill at the air at the stillness of it all
No one to yell at
No one to care
Dallas
I'm done with you

Shell of Independence

This child constructed a shell of independence
To manage the loneliness
The helplessness
The unfulfilled longing
This child developed a strategy to stop feeling stop
    longing
She decided
To live in a land of doing
It was her salvation
Until it was her prison
The doctor said
We all long
Long to love
Long to belong
Long to become
She gasped let out a sigh
She created a shell to keep herself safe
From her feelings
From the outside world
To stay unaware of her needs
But then it came
A crack in the shell
Let's let some love in said the little girl
I'm dying in here and so are you
The adolescent the adult the warrior tried to overrule
But the little girl was stronger than them all

She was going to get her way once and for all
She wouldn't have it any other way
She had waited too long
She wouldn't wait one more minute
She was done

My Name

Which one are you
What's your name little girl
The sound of those questions recede as I grow not to care
The sun knows my name
The wind knows my name
The trees know who I am
The horse that loved me never asked which one I was
She didn't care
She knew love didn't come in a name or a bottle
Today the wind blows through my mane just like it did hers
The ocean envelops my body
The grass bends under my feet
Who embraces your being
Who gravitates to your energy
Who is blinded by your light
It's not about I am
Or which one are you
When you discard the letters of your name
Do you know who you are?

Fragments of Me

They are everywhere
The fragments of me
In the closet in the drawer in the ceiling looking down
The fragments of me are all over the land
They are in Chicago
In Maryland
In the hall at my school
In my bedroom
Where I broke into two

What about you
Are you shattered
Are you fragmented
In pieces as well
Is your life here on earth
A heaven or hell
Do you vacillate
Between power and impotence
Wanting nothing or wanting it all
Do you stare down on yourself dissociated from life
When you close your eyes do you pray for the relief of a knife

Tell me tell me
Are you the coward the hero a player of hearts
Do you know who you are or have you vanished from your life
Stand up show yourself stop hiding here and there
Go pick up the pieces
They're everywhere

It's a mess it's a shambles
You are here and you are there
Don't you see
Don't you care that you're everywhere

It's up to you
Up to you to piece together your life
Up to you to make sense
Up to you to go back
Back to where it began
Go back to your birth
Go back if you can
Go back to Hyannis
Go back to your room
Go back

Tell him you know and no longer feel shame
Tell her you love her and pray for her pain
Go back pick up the pieces
Make yourself whole
Go back to the fragments
They're the key to your soul

Discovering

———

The Truth Dazzles Gradually

The truth dazzles gradually
Or the world would be blind
Said she
You need new eyes yes you do
As you cannot see what is
Make a way for yourself inside of yourself
Speak of your pain my child
The pain in between the places of your skin
Yes that place that defies words defies description defies the mind
You know it you feel it
Write to it
And remember this
To be alive is to breathe

Prepare yourself for the life that awaits you
Discover your truth
Dazzle your way forward
Day by day
Year by year
Remember the world would be blind if you dazzled all at once
So dazzle gradually
Open your eyes
See what is revealed

Intuition

As a child I had a sense
Of what was going on
But questions never yielded truth
And so a cloud set in

Clouds cloud intuition
Darkness settles in
It all begins to feel murky deep within
Once dissonance sets in
It's hard to trust your gut
But still I persevered
A sense was speaking up

As I look back over time and years
I realize my intuition
Has rarely taken me astray
It's I who have pushed it to the side
It's I who trampled its very truth
When I let it rise
Its ferociousness took my breath away

My intuition led me on a path
No map showed me where to go
But better that than denying what you know
Because disregarding your intuition
Can yield a fatal blow

The Cross

I have carried the cross long enough
I'm putting it down
It's heavy and I've carried it long enough
I'm strong enough to lift it off others
I want my own load to be lighter freer
I've got to rise up and I can't
With that heavy cross on my back
It's so painful to carry

Put it down
Put it down by the side of the road
Wherever you want to put it down
Put it down
It no longer serves any purpose
Put it down
By the side of the road in that fancy hotel
Wherever you want
Put it down
Because only then can you rise up
Only then can you unfold into your own becoming
Only then can you really do God's work here on earth
Only if you take the cross off your back
Only if you put it down

Cursed or Blessed

Cursed or blessed
Which one are you
The time will come when you'll have to decide
Decide which one are you
Are you like me
Who always felt the weight of the curse
The shame of being
Or are you one of those people
Who walk through life like it's a gift
Who smile and say good day
Those people can't really be that free that simple that blessed
Or can they?

I Am Both

Who am I
Sandy beaches or sold-out halls
Playing around or praying aloud
Passion unbridled or politics unrivaled
Running wild or being fenced in
Saving myself or saving the world
Sleeping in or sleepless days
All play and no work
All work and no play
Gentle touches or forceful toughness
A good girl or a little naughty
Making love or having sex
Dining with two hundred or dinner for two
Uncalm and unkempt or hairdresser on call
A cozy room
A sprawling house
Come closer
Go away
I see clearly
I don't know
Love me
Don't love me
Who am I
I am both
Or am I

What About You?

I live on many levels
What about you
Intense passionate fiery
Smart clever kind
Dark light strong weak
I live on so many levels
What about you

Do you shine only light
Do you feel only good
Are you calm all the time
Do you have just one self
What about you

Do you burn intensely bright
Do you love intensely big
Do you care way too much then not at all
Do you live on many levels
Do you hide behind many doors
Do you temper your intensity
Why do that

Be braver be brighter
The world can handle intense
Try it
Life is too short to not be that bright
But way too long to burn at that intensity
Delicate or intense
Which one are you

At First Sight

It happened just like that
At first sight
And you knew
Knew that nothing would ever be the same again
He smiled, laughed, looked you up and down
It happened before you knew
And then you did
It would take you from there to here
From love and freedom
To pain and prison
It would make you feel full, high on life
And make you feel alone and scared

It all happened at first sight
You fell
Fell hard
You would never ever really be able to reclaim your eyes
Or your heart
You could only do your best to regain your sight
Redirect your gaze and try again

It happened at first sight
You knew he knew
Neither of you would ever be the same because
What happens at first sight can never be unseen
You know what you know

Close your eyes these many years later
And you still recall that first sight

Your dress was blue
His suit was cream
The music was loud but then it slowed down
The room fell away
You knew he knew

It happened at first sight
Your eyes have never been the same nor will they ever be
Your heart open then broken
You know
You knew
When they say it happens at first sight
It's true

Really Truly

There are those moments in life that defy description
You know but just can't find the right words
I call them really truly moments
There are people in life who are really truly too
Sometimes they stand by you for a lifetime
Sometimes they are just passing through
You never know

All we know is that the really truly feeling stays inside of you
It was always inside of you
Because you are really truly
Really truly divine
Really truly good
Really truly unique
As in one of a kind
Rare
You my love are
Really truly enough
That's really true
Said me to you

The Wild in Me

Curious restless anxious that's me
Driven focused
Relentless can't you see
Can you sense what sounds these words muffle
What drive they suppress
These words camouflage what's going on inside
Oh my say you
What is that what can it be

Well my friend step back make sure you understand
Because there's a wildness in me
That no man can tame
There's a geyser underneath that won't be contained
Don't be fooled by the pretty dresses or the cross on my neck
Don't let the Mother Mary medals make you believe
I am more Virgin than Magdalene
More tame than wild

Step back watch your heart
Step forward if you dare
Consider yourself warned
There's a wildness in me that cannot be tamed

Crazy

Crazy crazy that's what you are
Crazy to think
Crazy to doubt
Crazy to believe
That's who you are
You're crazy
Crazy to wonder to see to feel
Crazy to question to act
And think that's real

Oh I wish I were
But it turns out I'm not
Not crazy in the head
Not crazy in the heart

Crazy no more
Taking my mind back from the edge
Crazy gives way
Crazy fades
In its place
Stands you
Stands one wild sane totally
Crazy me

No Needs

I feel like I've found some personal strength
Strength for me
In the past I've had strength on behalf of others
But it's been lacking when it came to me
When it came to my deserve
My worth
I realize now my needs are OK
They're not too much
I'm not too much

I've been pretending
I have no needs
But that's a lie
I've lied to myself and others only to resent
That no one saw my needs or attended to them
But how could they have known
I hid my needs from you and me
I pretended
I recoiled
I scoffed at those with needs
Including me

Knock Knock Open the Door

I awoke
Words came
You deserve
Your needs are not too much
It's not too much to expect that someone you love
Would open the door when you knock
Not too much to expect someone to answer the phone when
    you call
Not too much to need to want to ask

Your needs can be met by another
You can be met
The kind of love you need is coming
Not the kind you are used to
Not the kind you seek or run after
But the kind that will make you uncomfortable at first
That will make you weep over its gentleness
The kind of love that will make you break into tiny little pieces
So you finally can be put back together again
Knock knock
Open the door

Longing

Dear Life

I've been wanting to talk to you lately to tell you
You are not what I planned
You may not give a damn but I thought you should know
You are not what I expected
I thought as long as I had my compass pointing north
All would be good
But I learned that my heart doesn't know north
My life has led me on a path written in invisible ink
Longing for more from a soul I didn't know yet

So here we are Life
Without a compass without a map
Only my heart guiding me forward
It wonders
Am I ready to be known in a new and deep way?
Am I strong enough to open my heart and divulge what lies
    within?

Life you say that's what you are all about
Let's see how the universe responds
When I pull back the curtain on my soul

Wonder

I wonder do you see what I see
Do you marvel at the sun
Does the moon take your breath away
I wonder
Do you see beauty with your eyes
Or does your anxious mind only show you what is wrong
Wrong with the world
Wrong with you
Take my word
It's easier to see the world through God's benevolent gaze

Look at yourself
Look at who's looking at you
Can you tell
Can you feel
Can you see
Everywhere you look
You can choose to see beauty love possibility
Or destruction deprivation hopelessness

What do you see
Allow the mind to wander and wonder and see with God's eyes
Your thoughts will follow
If you choose to do that your life will change

What's keeping you from seeing yourself as a miracle
What's keeping you from seeing yourself as divine
What's keeping you from seeing yourself this way
You
Think about it

A Room Full of Grief

I lie in the room alone
The hotel is busy
Doors bang
Voices sound
I listen alone in my room

The phone doesn't ring
The TV is off
I have no one to call
No one to talk to
Or do I?

I lie in stillness in solitude
I weep
I want to feel my grief
Where does it come from
What does it tell me?

Grief floods me
I am no longer alone in the room
Grief has moved in quietly
I didn't hear it knock
The phone didn't ring

It was just there and everywhere
It engulfed me
Hello I said
I've been waiting for you a long time

I knew deep in my soul
One day you would come

You can have this moment
I will let you be
If in the end you leave me to be
Leave me to me

God, Are You Listening?

God, are you listening?
How many times
Have I asked you
Are you listening
Do you hear my whispers my cries my wails
Do you hear anything I say
Do you hear my rage
Do you read my mind
I speak to you most days
I don't want to bother you
Don't want to impose
But I wonder if you are listening

Can you hear my cries
Do you feel my pain
Can you sense my heartbreak
Can you help me with my sorrow
Can you ease my regret
Can you tell me where I'm going
If I'm going to be OK

God are you listening or keeping me at bay
I don't want to impose
I know you have a lot on your plate
But I'd love to know if you're listening
Listening to my prayers
To my whimpers to my tears
Can't you hear me asking what it is you want me to do

I don't hear your answers
God I can't hear your thoughts

Maybe you're just not listening
Maybe you just don't care
Maybe you're just too busy up there
But I'll keep talking
I'll keep praying because I have faith
Faith that are you listening
Listening to my prayers

The Hospital

The machines are loud
The needles bruise her arms
She is thin
She is frail
She is my mother

The hospital is a cold and lonely place
It is her home away from home
She does not complain
She is my mother

She is frail
She is weak
But she says she is fine
No problem here
She is my mother so she carries on pushes on
She is my mother

When it is time to go
I kiss her head
I know it's hard
I know she's sad
But she is my mother

Thank you, she says
You've been great
I leave my mother behind

Boston ICU

Where does this road lead with all its twists and turns
Which turn do I take
What role do I play
Do I let go
Do I step in
Do I sit and dream looking out the window at the river below
Or do I pretend that all is okay
All I know is that I don't know

With Mummy I write
We write together
"Your love has brought me to my knees
I can't breathe without you
I can't think without you
I'm lost without you
The clouds are clear
The sky is clear."

Then she says to me
"You are the trumpet of my life
You are the star of my life
The music in my step
You are the sunshine of my life."

Going Home

I sit on the plane
With heavy heart
Not sure where I belong these days
Not sure

My eyes well with tears
My lips tremble a bit
I can't see where I should go
Can't see where I should be
Don't know where I belong
Everywhere feels wrong

I close my eyes with the hope I will see
Exactly what life wants from me
I take a deep breath
Nothing is clear
How long will it be
Until I can see
Where I should be

I Came Back

I came back, even though you told me not to
I came back because it was unfinished
Did I tell you all I wanted to
Does anyone ever?

Thank you for giving me the breath of life
Thank you for giving me a push over and over again
Thank you for doing your best
I needed more but you couldn't have known
Neither could I

You did what you could with this wild and sensitive child
She wasn't you but you couldn't have known
You did what you could

So here we are
And now it's you needing the breath of life
Now it's you who needs the push
You did it for me so I'll do it for you
I've done what I could
I'll do what I can

What I Want

I want you with me when I die
I want your hands to close my eyes
I want your tears to clean my face
I want your arms to fold my hands
I want your voice to lift my soul
Out of the room and into the sky
There I will wait among the dead for you to come
There I will wait
Wait for you

Walk in the Water

The sun was blaring down
It was midday
I was walking
Walking to nowhere in particular
Just walking
Along the street by the ocean alone
I had walked it a thousand times before
As a child as a teenager and now as a woman

I buried you the day before
I was wandering and wondering
Thinking what will become of me
With you gone
I'd heard them say you cannot be the woman you are meant to be
Until your mother dies
So here I am a woman without a mother
Does that make me the woman I'm meant to be
Or just a bereaved daughter

Off in the distance I see another woman walking towards me
She is dressed not for the beach but for a special occasion
A long skirt white shirt and a simple cross
She carries a purse like you used to do
She walks straight up to me
And gives me five holy cards
Five holy cards
She says she is a former nun
A Missionary of Charity

She asks me Have you been in the water today
What?
She takes my hand
And together fully dressed we walk into the water
Walk into the ocean

Only you my mother would do such a thing
Only you my mother went into the water dressed in clothes
Now here am I standing in the ocean fully clothed
Holding the hand of a total stranger in a skirt and a blouse
A woman from you or from God
I don't know
It doesn't matter

This woman who just appeared took me into the water to be
    blessed
To be baptized to become a woman
For me for my family I walked into the water
To become the woman I am

You led me there
You held me there
You came back so I would know you were OK
And that I could become the woman I could only become once
    you left
My mother in heaven and on earth you came back
Back to me
Thank you

I Know You Loved Me

Beyond a shadow
Beyond the words
Beyond the picture of what a loving nurturing mother
Is supposed to look like
Act like
Talk like
Touch like
There is you

I couldn't find anyone like you in my picture books
No mothers looked like you
Dressed in pants like you
Had hair like you
Played football like you
Smoked cigars like you
Yet I knew you loved me

I knew you wanted more for me than you had been given
I knew you wanted for me everything you had been denied
Beyond a shadow I know you loved me
The way you smiled at me and cheered for me
The way you pushed me
I know you loved me
Do you know how much I loved you
Beyond a shadow you were my everything

I understand so much more about you today
You too were scared
You too longed to be seen

You too longed to be held
My heart breaks for you
As I've come to learn we cannot give what wasn't given to us

As you grew older you softened
You allowed me in
My heart breaks for my mother
But no one let her in
But no one held her
No one comforted her
No one told her she was enough

Her journey was relentless
Her energy unbridled
I understand now and I'm so sorry

Beyond a shadow I know you loved me
Beyond a shadow I loved you

Deep Inside

Don't you understand that longing isn't love
Love fills you up
Longing aches longing illuminates what is missing
Thirst longs for water
The bud longs for the sun
The dog longs to be pet to be met to be loved
You long for what was
For your father's brain to be what it was not what it is
Sharp like a knife clear as water as vast as the ocean
The stories it held the knowledge it contained all gone
Like grains of sand on the beach the stories sift thru your fingers
Imagine what it's like for him
There is nothing left or is there
Who knows what lurks within
The unknowing the knowing all are one
Who are you he says
I am Maria your daughter
And the light within his eyes flashes
A smile crosses his face
Oh wow says he
I always wanted a daughter named Maria

Missing

There it is again
It sneaks up
Floods you like a heavy rain
It's pouring
Pouring down
Down all around

I'm missing you
Missing your smile
Your laugh your eyes
I'm missing you
Missing the names you called me
The way we are the way you are
The way you were as a child
I'm missing you
Missing your love that's what it is

So I close my eyes and I remember
Remember how you held my hand
How you called my name
I remember your smile your goofy ways
I remember your heart
The way you made me feel

So know that wherever you go
I'll be missing you
But also know that wherever you go you are here
    with me

Right here next to me
Right here in my heart
Right here in my mind
The missing gives way to the loving
Loving that I'm missing you

Revealing

Revelation

It ripped thru me like a tornado
So forceful I had to sit down
The revelation that Calcutta was in me
Once I said the words aloud
The tears sprang up
For the first time I didn't try to push them away
I wanted to stay in it
The poverty the slums the abandonment
It was in me
In me all along
The Calcutta I've been searching for is inside of me
The pain of it made me dizzy
It felt like too much

Within moments pieces of the puzzle started falling into place
No wonder my own mother was drawn to Mother Teresa
She too was looking somewhere deep in herself
She knew
Knew she too was a forgotten child
Knew she too was abandoned
Knew she too was looking for mother love
Someone to hold her care about her love her
She thought her Calcutta was in institutions
But she herself was the one locked away
She couldn't slow down couldn't pause
It was too painful
My heart breaks for the little girl inside my raging mother

. . .

That little child in me is broken starving poor alone
I'm Calcutta
I'm an orphan
I'm an addict

No wonder I felt pulled to the nuns
They are mothers
No wonder I went to the orphanage in Delhi
And was confronted by a young nun named, yes, Maria
Tender, caring
I met me
I pick up the child in me in all of us
I am here to mother
I am here to care
I am here to tend to the sick in each of us

Those orphans are in big houses and fancy restaurants
They are hiding everywhere

My Calcutta is inside of me
Mother Teresa Mummy me Maria
I'm integrating mother and child
I'm making myself whole

I was left in the apartment
In the crib in the empty room
I was left in the elevator, in the halls of power
The streets of Tunisia the fields of Senegal
The hut on the reservation
The igloo on the banks of the frozen river
The pieces of me are everywhere
Pieces of me left for someone to pick up

That someone is me
That is my calling

To Mother
To love
It's not what I thought but it's what I need
Mother love
Pick up the pieces
That's what mothers do
They pick up the pieces
Of you

Cherished and Shamed

Loved and rejected
Adored and disliked
Cherished then shamed
Paradoxes everywhere
Isn't that interesting
Isn't that something

Pay attention
Those conflicting things can go together
You are not crazy
To feel both
To think Hey what's happening here

One moment there is love adoration attention
The next coldness neglect invisibility
They go together these things
They shouldn't but they can

Run for your life if you feel them notice them
You are not crazy
You see what is
Now run for your life

Beneath the Confusion

I am confused I told the woman
Confused about this
Confused about that
She listened nodding her head
I continued looping around saying this saying that
She listened
Eventually I stopped
Exhausted by my own confusion
Confused by my own unknowing

Then calmly she spoke
You are not confused
The confusion you profess she said
Is the denial of your own truth
Silence
I stared
She stared back
Beneath your confusion she continued is your knowing
I went to speak
Stop she said
Be quiet
Rest listen wait
Silence
Then like a siren she snapped
Truth
Say it
Say what you know to be true
Don't think

Just say the first thing that comes to your mind
Truth
Say your truth

You know
You know you are beautiful, that your truth is real
You know you are worthy, that your light is bright
You know it isn't right to dim it all just to be safe
Your fear is making you doubt
Your fear is driving your mind
Your fear is all over your body
You are so afraid
Afraid to say no when you know
Afraid to say stop when you know

You are afraid you will die
Afraid you can't go on
You are afraid of others
Their words
Their stares
Their judgments
You are afraid you're not smart enough
Not good enough
Not quiet enough
You are right
You are not
You know
You know you don't belong here
You know your voice is strong
You know this time is over
You know
So go

And so beneath the confusion
There it was
My knowing
My truth
Out it came
Clear as a glass of water

Stop Trying to Make Life Make Sense

Like you I've tried so hard to make sense of this life
My life
I've searched I've struggled
I've beaten myself up
I've longed and learned I've listened and spoken
I've wept I've laughed I've questioned
And then done it all over again

I've tried on happiness
I've tried on victimhood sainthood
Martyrdom leadership
Nothing really made sense
I tried tying my ship to another
It sailed for a while until I also wanted to put my hand on
    the tiller
That's when the sea got rocky and turned over the ship
I treaded water for a long time
Trying to get everyone to safety
Once I did I realized I was still treading

Life
How do I handle you
I've been told to swim against the tide
Been told to float
Been told to dive in and come out the other side
Been told to tame the rapids
And just let them take me
Take me downstream

Stop fighting the current the pull
I'm told
Ride it out and let it guide you to shore
Oh really

This thing called life
It doesn't make sense
One minute you are
Strong solid
Then
Fragile breakable
Insecure uncertain

———

That's where I have landed
In uncertain terrain
Uncertain is where I am
Uncertain about you
Uncertain about me
Uncertain where I belong or if I do
It's not about you it's about me

The walls are up the brakes are locked
Uncertain said he
Oh my said she
Hello goodbye
Uncertain said he
Yes said she
I stand in the uncertainty of this thing called life
I stand in the unknowing
Fragile and strong
Scared and confident
That I will find my way

Who am I talking to
The me in me the me in you
My fragmented self
There is no you
Just different parts of me

The self
It's feminine it's masculine
It's forceful domineering submissive and soft
It's feminine loving and nurturing
It steps out in the world and retreats
Power-hungry
Peace-loving
Fractured ordered
Wild and creative
Sane and mad

Breathe, self
Integrate
Stop trying to make sense
Stop trying to be sane
Rest in your insanity
Stop fighting your madness

Life brings it all to the forefront
You are beautiful
Powerful light and yes sane

Life
Your madness just made sense of your sanity
Now rest where you are
Strong sane with a touch of madness
Ha!

The Uninvited Guest

That's what you are
You show up unannounced and just walk right in
You wander around my mind like it's yours
Turning things upside down after I'd gotten them just so
Throwing things around

I'm so tired of your visits
I'm so tired of the way I feel after you've shown up
Tired numb listless
You make me want to give up
Go back to my room
I try to shut you out but you keep banging at my door
You are the uninvited guest
You stay way too long

This time I'm going to rise up kick you out
And ask you not to come back again
I know you will
But I'll rise up again and again
Until it will be you who ends up feeling tired numb listless

I can't wait until you go
Why should I wait until you want to go
Let me show you the door
Out you go
Don't come back
You are not welcome here anymore
You are the uninvited guest
And from now on I'm inviting in only who I want to

One Day

So much of life is spent in anticipation of one day
One day I'll get that job
One day I'll take that trip
One day I'll buy that home
One day she will call
One day he will come back
Then one day you're sitting there looking at the sky and you
    realize
That one day is but a fantasy
One day is just a hope a thought
One day isn't real
You stop looking up and just look straight ahead
Not to one day but to today
Today is all you have
All you have to say is what needs to be said
Do what needs to be done
One day is today
Don't trade today for one day
Because one day may never come

Choose

You can make a choice
And yet you don't
So terrified are you of making the wrong one
Choices will be made by you or for you
Choose to go or to stay
To go back or go forward
To the left
To the right
Choose
Choose your thoughts
Choose your future
Choose
But if I choose where will I go
You don't get to know
You just must choose
A strong woman chooses
She steps forward
She stands in her choice with all its uncertainty
Decisions
Choices
Choosing
There they are
Choose

Chaos

Life can unfold into chaos
Before you know its name
You can live in it and with it and not know it
Not realize you are addicted to it
It creeps up on you
You drink it
Get high on it
It flows through your veins
Making you feel alive
And then you crash when it's gone

In the midst of chaos
You behave in ways you had no business behaving
You stand up for things you now see
You had no business standing up for
You say things you look back on and wonder why
Why you said it
Why you did it
Why you lived like that

Chaos what a mistress you are
I'm finally ready to break up with you

Picture Perfect

I thought I had it all
Or so it seemed to me
The picture I painted in my head looked beyond perfect to me

I've come to understand that there is no such thing
Perfect is what we tell ourselves
What we long to project
Perfect is just an illusion that covers up the cracks
So afraid are we of what we cannot see
That we attach to picture perfect
And just let it be

Perfect is what we tell others
So they look and wonder why
Why they don't have perfect in their eyes

The truth is no one ever lives a perfect little life
We all have cracks and fissures
Life is just like that
But I must say for me
I thought I had it all
Or at least enough to suffice
That is
                    Until my perfect ran out of time

Heartache

Time Stood Still

There are those moments when time stands still
You have no words
The room might move
You may lose your balance
Get dizzy feel faint
You look around but you cannot see
It was like that for me.
I heard the words
But I had dissolved
I wasn't there.
The me that returned wasn't the same me
She was gone
The woman looking in the mirror was a stranger
She tilted her head this way and that
Straining to connect.
Nothing
The moment changed everything
Nothing was ever the same again

The Truth

They say the truth is the thing that sets us free
In reality I think not
I think it breaks hearts
Evaporates dreams
Ravages families
Destroys lives

I understand why so many run from the truth
It beckons us to it and then leaves us
Sitting there in our destruction

It tells us we will feel better but we don't
It tells us it will set us free but it doesn't
Truth: Are you an angel or the Devil?

Broad Beach

The rain pounds down
The ocean doesn't care
It just rolls in
Wave after wave
It pays no heed to the rain

I can hear it clink-clank in the gutter pipe
I wish I were like the ocean
I wish I could just roll in
Crash down
I can't

I wish I were like that bird I see
Flying back and forth across the sky
Unperturbed by the rain
Unaffected by the waves
It just floats by

Why can't I float by like the bird
Roll in like the wave
Pound down like the rain
Or break through like the sun
Yes I'm like the sun
Struggling to break through

The rain stops
The birds are gone
The waves still roll

I want the sun to break through
I imagine that it has
But reality reminds me that all too often
I lie to myself
Too scared am I of the truth

Ring Ring

Ring ring
Ring ring jump
Jump
Every time I heard the sound
Terror filled my body
My heart raced
My throat froze
Ring ring
I dared not pick it up
What tragedy lurked behind the ring
What news would shatter me yet again
Ring ring pick me up it cried
Ring ring slowly I moved towards its sound
I took a breath I steadied myself
Ring ring
I stood there body intact
But I had left the room
Ring ring

The Public Square

Shame filled my body
Humiliation filled my soul
Every inch of my being crumbled
I stood humbled disgraced mortified in the public square
I heard the whispers
How could she not have known
Not have seen
She must have
She couldn't have not
Poor her
Poor them
I could feel the stares
Of pity of scorn
I tried to meet them but
Eyes turned away
I stood in the public square a mere shadow of my former
    self
Until I thought
No
This is not how it's going to go
I'm going to rebuild
I'm going to discard
I'm going to stand in all that I am
And carry on
Move forward

Make no mistake
I hear you I see you
But
You'll see
Your whispers have nothing on me

Rejection

I was just sitting
Sitting there in the early morning light
The window cracked half-open
The coffee brewing
The dog snuggled up on the chair
My mind was on the day ahead but my heart was aching
Tugging at that feeling from the other day

You know what I'm talking about
Don't play naïve
Don't pretend you don't know
Don't pretend it didn't cut
Face it
That familiar feeling of rejection
It cuts
It makes you wince
Makes you pitch forward
Rejection
You focus so intently on the one rejecting you
The why of it all
The why

Then like a crack of light it hits
The tears start flowing
What is this
Is it from him again
No it's the overwhelming realization
That the one rejecting you is not him
It's you
You you you

A gasp comes out of your small mouth
Oh oh oh
You moan
Moan in pain
Say it isn't so
You moan
The tears flow
But it is
It is exactly what you know it to be

You reject you
That's why you tried to find someone to accept you

It was only then you felt OK
But that gave your power away
That gave your worth away
That gave you away
It's not about him
Not about her
It's about you

Stop rejecting you
Stop stop stop
Look in your eyes
Accept what you see
Then no one can reject you ever again
Accept accept accept
Or moan your life away

Fear

I can feel it all over my body
The cloak of fear and shame
I want it off but I can't get it off
It's so heavy this coat
I sense that underneath it is freedom
But I can't get it off

Fear
I feel it in my chest my shoulders down into my legs
Fear is all over my body
I hate my body I want to love it
My desire to love it is greater than my hatred
My longing to love is greater than my hatred of me
I've been trying to save us ever since I was little

I tried screaming out
No one heard
I tried going up and down in the elevator looking for help
I couldn't find anyone
I ran through the hotel in Washington yelling
No one came
In the house in Maryland I banged on the doors I jumped up and
    down Help help help
Somebody help us
My mother is not here
The nanny is bad my father is weak my brothers are crying
Help help someone anybody help us
. . .

Mummy can't you see we are dying out here
Please get up please come please don't die
I need you to save us or tell me you can't so I can get us help
I'll go looking to find us a man
A man who can help us

I looked and I found one I found one
He can help us for a while
Yes he did but then I realized that he couldn't
Now I was really scared I knew I needed help
I ran around yelling
I need doctors I need nurses
Don't you see we are in danger we're in danger yes we are yes
      we are
We need help
I'll go looking I'll go searching
I'll find us the one

I can't save you my father I can't save you my mother
I don't want to be saved she said
My brothers are asleep I can't wake them it's true

I realized I need to save myself
Does anyone hear me does anyone see the horror I'm living
I'm exhausted from trying to find someone
But I'll keep screaming keep crying keep asking
Is it you is it you

The fear in my house was enormous
I was searching and spying and trying to find out what was true
I told a few people I felt that I knew
I made arrangements to get myself out
I hid in the hotel hoping no one found out

I stayed in the corner shaking it's true
I knew I was in danger

I'm afraid I'm afraid but I know there is nothing anyone can do
My kids they came over
I was safe it is true
No one can harm us
This I knew
Then I moved us to a home I settled my kids
I did this alone so that no one knew

Turns out that the screaming the crying was all just for me
To get me to step up and save us
I never stopped trying
I'm sorry it's true
I'm the hero of this story I brought us all home
I was there with my mother my father as well
I drove away from the hell
I found a safe place and made it my own
I got us out I got us safe
It only took a lifetime of longing and of loss
I'm no longer in danger
No longer in fear
I'm safe and I did it
I can exhale the fear

Stay

In an instant I realized leaving was no longer an option
There was nowhere left to go
You had traveled far into the future and the past
It was all circles and gloom
So unaware were you that you were the one who wouldn't
    couldn't stay

You sought out diversions and escapes
Fantasies and dreams
All so you wouldn't have to stay
Stay in your life in your body
In your present
Until you were swirling in anesthesia

It dawned on you to be quiet to focus your mind on silence
On you your body your present your pain
No more escaping to the stables to your room to your office
    to your work
No more escaping into other people's lives
So you don't have to feel your own

Come home to you and stay
Stay here
Stay with me
Let me heal your wounds
I know how tired you are how small you feel
How scared and wretched you are
I know how ashamed humiliated broken dissociated you are

I know the go part of you can't face the part that needs
    to stop
Stay still stay
There is nowhere left to go
Stay in your body
Stay in your heart
Stay in you
Stay home
It's where your salvation starts

Connecting the Dots

Before you deal with his betrayal the man counseled
You must first deal with your own
A betrayal that happened long ago
Perhaps you were not even aware
But somewhere along the way you betrayed yourself
It started small and slow then it grew

The woman was confused by the shaman's words
You could not be where you are today
Had you not betrayed yourself long ago he whispered
Small betrayals of the self lead you to a place
Where you no longer know yourself
Where you no longer have the ideals you once did
The values you say you do
Or do you

Is that why you are here trying to connect the dots
Look back think back
Connect the dots that brought you here
Reflect on all the small betrayals
Dot by dot
Look at how you lied to yourself deceived yourself
Dot by dot
Look at where you denied what you knew to be true
Dot by dot
Lie by lie
You allowed others to decide what was
Even though it conflicted with what you felt believed knew

Dot by dot
You gave up gave in
Until you accepted what you never would
Until you were so confused
You did not know who you were

Dot by dot you reclaimed yourself
Dot by dot
You have put the pieces of your life together
You have learned
It isn't about the other
It's always about your own path
Everything and everyone is here to teach you a lesson
Have you learned it
Can you see it can you feel it

Forgive yourself
Reclaim yourself
It isn't about the other
It's always about you
Dot by dot

I Want to Give Up

I want to give up
Lie down
Call it a day
I'm tired of trying
Trying to find my way

Don't you see that I'm lost
That I can't soldier on
Does anyone else know what's going on

Do others feel this way
Or am I the only one
The only one who wants to call it a day

I look ahead and see so much wide open space
With which I know not what to do
I'm tired I'm sad
And the truth is
I have not a clue

No clue where to go
Not a clue what to do
No clue who to talk to
Not a clue
What about you?

Do you feel what I feel
Are you tired or lost
Or do you pretend

That you know
Exactly what to do?

I'll carry on
Try to smile
Do my best
But the truth of the matter is
I just want to rest

I want to lie at your feet
I want to stop all the noise
Give up give in
And call it a day
But you know that I won't
No I won't
Call it a day

I'll try again tomorrow
I'll try to stand tall
But the truth is I'm so afraid that I'll fall

So God please show me the way
Show me where I belong
Show me who cares
Please don't take long
I'm tired but I'm ready
So please God
Show me the way

Today God Said to Me

Today God said to me
Follow me
Stay focused stay present
Stop looking around for someone to love you or for you to love
Stop it
It's wasting your energy
Love isn't like that
Stop looking for it

Ease into your own being
Ease into you
Lower your intensity
Lower your vibration
Ease into yourself
Ease into me

Stop looking to others to love you like you want to be loved
They can't
So stop asking
Stop waiting and wanting
Stop trying
Leave it be

Put blinders on and carry forward
Get a warm towel and wrap your heart up in it and take it back
Hold on to it safely securely and solidly
You've got it

You can do this
Hold on to your heart until it's healed
It's hurt be gentle with it
But you can heal it
You are the only one who can

I Wonder

When I hear your name I wonder
Wonder how you are
Where you are
What you are thinking
I wonder are you happy
I wonder are you sad
I wonder do you think of me
I wonder do you wonder about me
Do you remember me
My laugh my voice my dreams my hopes
Do you remember my body
The mane that is my hair
Do you remember my eyes their color their joy their longing
What it was like to look deep into them
Do you do you remember anything about me
I wonder
If you wonder

Betrayal

You search around your mind and heart for the why of it
You keep coming up empty
Like a bucket searching for water in an empty well
Like a squirrel running to find food that isn't to be found
The man you pleaded with to help you shakes his head
He lays it out
You betrayed you long before anyone else could
You have the power to forgive yourself heal yourself pardon
    yourself repair yourself
Well then
Go back in time to the smallest transgressions to the smallest lies
    you Told yourself to the betrayals you thought just this time
    just this once
No one will know see or care
Aww my child, but it all adds up until you don't know yourself
    anymore You doubt yourself in that moment
You allow the biggest of transgressions to occur until you stop and
    see That you are the bird the squirrel the empty bucket
You bowl over, ashamed at what you have allowed and then you
    rise Up and scream so that the heavens break up
The rain fills the bucket
The worm drops into the bird's mouth the squirrel stores nuts in
    his mouth and you
You are alive in your own body
In charge of your own mind
The animal instinct kicks in and off you run into the forest never
    to be betrayed again

A Fall Evening

The sun is setting
The rays shine on a path
Across the ocean's belly

The waves crash across it
But the sparkle doesn't move
It's God's show for me

I sit here alone on this fall evening
Looking
Breathing
Aching

I ache all over as I watch dogs play in the waves
I ache all over as I watch couples walk arm in arm
I ache to sit here alone
Alone with my heart
With my tormented mind

I settle with the pain
The loneliness
I soak it in so I know what I no longer want to feel
As the sun sets
I hope it takes my pain with it

The Storm

You are standing in it
Unsure of how to survive
It blows past every part of you
You breathe to calm your racing heart
You choke on tears that won't stop
You try to hold your ground but feel it slipping away

When will the wind stop
When will the rain let up
When will the leaves stop falling the branches stop breaking
When will the howling subside
When will there be light
You scream for answers
The storm laughs at you
And just rages on
It's on its own path of destruction
You are in the way
You can stand and fight it
Or you can step aside
And let it pass
Let it go
Let it be

You do
And the rage blows by
The rain moves on
The wind finds another
And slowly you see light is breaking through
You survived
Again

Healing

———

Be Miracle-Minded

Your mind wages war on your tender little heart
You know that don't you child
Said the voice from afar
So instead be miracle-minded
Yes miracle-minded
I like the sound of that
But just how does that work
How does miracle-minded
Feel inside the busy mind

See yourself as the miracle you are
Said the soft voice
Look at nature
See that flower bursting forth
Look at the animals that meet your eyes
That hold your gaze
Aren't they too
Just like you
Miracles
Yes said you

You are alive
As is your spoken word
Don't be afraid of the dark
Don't be afraid to let what's in your mind out into the
     light of day

See everything this way
Your path will clear

I lay down the mind that fought me so long
I push thru the darkness into the light
I pick up my miracle mind and go on my way

Deserve

You deserve to be seen
To be respected adored
Say what?
Who's talking
Who's talking to me

It's me talking to the woman on the side of the road
To the man begging for money to feed his soul
To the kid in the foster home
It's me talking to them
Or is it me talking to me

What do you deserve
To be treated kindly and respectfully
Then start doing that
Stop judging stop driving stop the war with your body and
    your mind
Stop the war between your heart and your head that drives you
    to panic
Stop criticizing your every move and thought
Stop it stop it stop it

You are safe now
Safe to be
Safe to open your eyes to what is
Safe to let it all come tumbling down
It already has
And you didn't die

Because now isn't your time
Now you deserve to live
Live free live in peace
Live
It's up to you
You deserve to

It Became Clear to Me

It became clear to me
That I have been groping grasping for your attention your love
Trying over and over
Trying to be wanted
Trying to be enough
Trying not to be too much
Trying to be quiet not too smart
Trying to be what someone wants
I've tried to dim my light
I've tried to be and do so many things
But most of all I keep trying to be in an epic love story

I realize now at the end of the summer that I must simply stop
Stop cold
Stop grasping and groping
Stop trying and hoping
Stop fantasizing
Stop needing
Stop trying to make someone like you love someone like me
I have learned
You can't make someone love you
I can't make someone come to me
And I can't stop someone from leaving
No matter how powerful clever or smart I think I am
It doesn't work so stop
. . .

And now let me state clearly to myself
Yes now I'm talking to you Maria
I see you
I see you with God's eyes
You are good you are fun funny creative curious
Smart sassy evolved and alive
Yes you are so alive
You are love
You are loving
You are nurturing
You are gracious generous and welcoming to others
You have felt "other" you have felt invisible and alone
So you reach out to others who you think might feel the same way

I believe in God and I believe that God made me to feel love
And to help others feel loved too
I am here to be of service

To feel safe secure seen and soothed to feel protected
And to feel worthy

To feel special
All of these things are what I've wanted to feel
I thought success would make me feel these things but it didn't

Being in conversation with others made me "feel"
Music made me "feel"
Someone saying something kind and real to me made me "feel"
It's ironic that I spent my life trying not to feel and now all I
    want to do
Is feel feel feel
Feel centered feel calm feel peaceful

Feel seen feel loved feel connected
Feel feel feel
I want to get out of my head and feel everything
I want to feel alive
Because I am

Dizzy

Dizzy
I feel dizzy
I almost couldn't stand up
I felt myself going back to that place
Disassociating dizzy
Sick to my stomach

It was a beautiful day
Walking back I looked to the ocean then looked to the road and
    then I saw him and his friend on bikes riding along
Riding right by me
Should I yell I thought
Say it's me Maria
I opened my mouth
Nothing came out
I just stopped walking and watched
I let him go
I let him go by

He didn't stop
Didn't even see me
Did I know deep down that even if I yelled out he would keep
    going?
He wouldn't stop
He wouldn't hear me
Or did I know that it no longer mattered
I didn't need him to stop
I didn't need him to acknowledge me
. . .

He just kept going
I stopped
The world started to spin
I looked for a bench to sit down afraid I'd fall
Breathe Maria breathe Maria

He was riding
Riding with an intensity
Only looking straight ahead
He didn't see me
Maybe he never has
Maybe he has never seen me
Or maybe he did
And knew deep down that he couldn't stop
He couldn't get off his bike

If he did maybe he would die
He wouldn't be him anymore

And somewhere I finally knew that it was wrong to ask him
    to stop
To stop get off and stay

He can't
It's not his fault it's not mine
I need to sit on the bench
Which is what I'm doing and look out at the ocean
He needs to keep biking
Pushing driving going forward
He can never stop
Now my back is to the road
I'm looking out at the ocean straight ahead
I'm alone on the bench

I'm dizzy I start to cry
I don't care who sees me
I sob
But I'm OK
I'm looking straight ahead
I'm alone but I'm OK
A couple walks by
They are holding hands
I know what I need to do
I reach for my own hand
I hold it
I'm OK

Buried Inside

It happened when I was sitting
Meditating
For the first time I could feel someone within me screaming
    to get out
As though she were buried in a coffin shouting yelling
Banging on the walls
Help help help let me out
I was still very very still
I didn't move I couldn't
My God that's me I said in my mind
I'm screaming to get out
My self is buried deep below the ground locked away in
    a box buried

I did it
Why I'm not sure
Or am I
To keep her safe to keep her quiet
Maybe both
But why?
Did I believe that she wouldn't be able to survive
That she would be too fragile tender emotional
That she was too small?

For the first time in my life I realized
What I had done
I had taken a part of me and split it off
And there she was
For the first time I could hear the screaming the yelling the
    pounding

I could sense the rage the anger
I felt this person was banging on walls
Suffocating screaming

I felt like I was going to throw up
Was I throwing her up?
Was I throwing up the other me?
I was sick to my stomach
I felt dizzy

I turned inward I reached down
I opened the latch
No wonder I've struggled to be heard
I haven't heard myself

No wonder I've been frustrated banging on the walls
It was me all along raging at myself
I've been yelling
Listen to me hear me let me out
I've been afraid of my gentle tender self the feeling me
I buried her to save her
No doubt she's angry
Deservedly so

I'm so sorry
Please forgive me
I finally hear you
It's safe come out
Now.

Cry for Love

Don't you see that everything in life is a cry for love
Don't you know that you must accept
Everyone in your life for who they are
Not for who you want them to be but for who they are
Don't you know control doesn't work
Stop trying to control
Stop it before it controls you
Don't you know that only love works

Everyone in your life is playing the role they are meant to play
When you shift everyone around you shifts
When you love really love everyone else is free to love
Not love of power
Not love of control

We are emotional hoarders we human beings
Yes we are hoarding emotions
Good ones and destructive ones
It allows no space for love to get in
You can't find it amidst the rubble
You can't see it amidst the mess
You can't feel it because you are hoarding all the stuff
That makes you believe it's not there for you
Everyone is crying out for love in messy ways
Angry ways dysfunctional ways

So clear yourself out
Tidy up that mess inside
Make room for the love

The real love
The love everyone is really crying out for
The kind of love that makes your heart feel full
The kind of love that just makes you smile
The kind of love that's there for everyone
Trust me it's there
It just can't get through

The Bench

My breathing is labored
As it slows I pause
It's been almost two years to the day
I'm sitting on a green iron bench
I feel alone
But now I look to my left
And I see there is room for another on my bench
And there is also another bench right next to mine
It's empty but there's room
Room for more in my life
I can fill it with whomever I want

There is a bench next to mine
There is a trash can next to my bench for all the garbage of my life
I can throw all the garbage out
I can get up without it

I'm not ready to stand up yet
I'm still lightheaded
But I now know there is room on my bench
Room next to my bench and an entire ocean in front of me

I pause
I'm healthy
My kids are healthy
I can fill the benches
I can get up when I'm ready
I can walk on
. . .

I feel the urge to bend over put my head between my legs
Just like a crash landing
The blood rushes to my head
I look down at my sweatshirt
It says HOPE in big letters
It says HOPE and my shirt underneath says UNFORGETTABLE
This moment this day this bench this feeling
Hopeful
Unforgettable

I'm ready to get up
I take a deep breath
I'm ready to walk on
And so I do

The Berkshires

The clouds hang over proud trees
Rain falls slowly
Gray mist envelops not just the space around my heart

I awake and my throat is blocked
What do I want to say and to whom
I know but still I cannot form the words
They are cloaked in mist and fog

This is where those old souls came to find their awe
Thoreau Emerson
What made their hearts stop
I don't care
What makes my heart stop
What makes my heart finally my own
The quiet makes my heart stop the breathing calms my mind
The gray lifts
The mist fades away

I know what I want to say
Go away leave me be
You had your way
You used me and I gave myself away
Well I want me back
Go away
I'm surrounded by the strong powerful trees
Go away
I'm here now
Go away

The mist is gone the clouds fall away
I'm here now it's my heart I feel
It beats and beats and beats

A bird flies by she flaps her wings she soars
Go away
I'm flapping my wings
I'm leaping
It's my day to soar

Regina Laudis

There you were
It was dawn
I stood there in the field and I knew
I felt it deep in my gut
It traveled up through my body and my eyes welled with tears
I knew
I stood there strong, centered
Sure it was clear
For the first time in my life everything else fell away and I knew
I had found you
You weren't on a red carpet
You weren't in the things, awards, photos, plaques
You weren't hiding under some red-soled shoes
Or in a fancy red leather box
I looked for you in clothes in accomplishments in men
How did you elude me

I traveled all over the world searching
You were there inside of me
No makeup no fuss nothing fancy
Just you
You were who I was looking for
And there you were in an Open Field at Regina Laudis
Where women go to be with God
Sheer love pared down to nothing

I found you at dawn
I brought you in

I hugged you
Now that I've found you I'll never let you go
I will never let another mistreat you another person degrade you
I'm sorry I didn't protect you better but I didn't know
You are safe
You are here
Thank you for stopping
Thank you for resting
For standing in one place long enough
So I could see you meet you love you
Welcome home

Forgiveness

Eleven letters
Eleven hundred tries
Over and over
The path to making that word a reality twists and turns

Eleven letters form that powerful word
Practice it
Preach it
Wrestle it down
Please he pleaded
That was easy
But forgiving oneself your self
Now that was/is hard
Brutal but necessary
How do you forgive for all that you did
How do you forgive for what you know not

On the legendary cross Jesus shouted out
Father forgive them for they know not what they did
Forgive them
Forgive him
Forgive her
None of us knows what we did
None of us should be forgiven
But all of us are

Thank you God for answering that plea
From the cross where we all hang at one time or another
Forgive them Father

Forgive me Father
I knew not
I knew yes
I knew
I know and yet I ask
I ask for forgiveness
For my small self my weak self
My self that sought home in all the wrong ways
If I forgive me
I can forgive him
I can forgive her
And so it is
All is forgiven
We are all free to go

Eleven letters eleven hundred thousand million tries
And then in an instant all is forgiven

Eleven letters
All hard-earned
Forgiveness

Shadow

Stop following me everywhere I go
Don't you know your name
Don't you know your place
Your menacing gaze
Your twisted face
Go away
Go back to the dark
You are not me and I no longer know your name
Cast off the old
That cloak no longer bears my name

See the needy child alone in the darkened corner
Crying out
Weak soiled alone
She beckons yet you resist
Arms outstretched
You dare not yield
Afraid for what it says about you
Her cries give way to muffled whimpers
You hate weak
You are disgusted by needy
Repulsed by the unmet cries of little me
Therein lies your shadow
Shadow you shadow me

And so a lifetime of ignoring needs wants desires
Of muffling cries
Best to kill the desire than let it go

Unheard let it go
Untamed shadow there you are
You've been hidden so long
I didn't even know your name
Instead I borrowed one that wasn't mine

Shadow I thought you were Anger Force Power
A tornado of energy to be contained
Alas you were the exact opposite
You are a baby's whimpers
You are a little girl's need
You are unmet love
You are emptiness
No one heard your cries

It's true no one cared enough for you
So you closed that door
You buried that girl
Determined she would never show her name her face
So determined were you to bury her heart
You did what you must do

But then lo and behold somehow she broke through
Somehow you heard her call
You stopped listened felt
What is that
Who is that

You came back so you could know her name
You came back to soothe her cries
You came back so she would know she's not alone
The room may be dark
The crib may be cold

But you
Your heart is open
Your embrace is vast
Your strength is real
You pick her up
You calm her down
You assure
You hold
You soothe
You mother
You feed her love
It's the only food we cry out for

The shadow falls
The need is met
You take her home
You came back for her
You are whole
You are home

Taking My Heart Back

I want to take my heart back
And put it in a place of honor
I want to revere it take care of it
But I need to be gentle with it
It's fragile
I want to love it back to fullness
Love it back to health
I start today

I need to protect it but not close it off
I need to show it but not put it in danger
Where it can be abused or taken advantage of
It's vulnerable
Vulnerable to a man coming along
Telling it a story creating a fantasy

I am in charge of my heart
I know what makes it feel good
My heart needs connection
It needs safety acceptance gentleness
It needs to be strongly held but not suffocated
It is now my most valued asset
My highest priority
I am in charge of loving my heart

Come back to me my heart
You work
You're okay
You can shine now
You're safe

Check the Box

The paper has several boxes
Single married divorced or widowed
Check one
You think it's clear don't you
But to me it isn't

The lady asks which one are you
She waits
Looking at you confused
Such an easy question
Such a complicated response

What if you feel like all four?
You are single but still feel married
You wore the D like a scarlet letter
But feel more like a widow

Single married divorced widow
That's who you are
A little of each
Who would have thought
Certainly not me

The Power of Faith

It happened in church
As it always does
You speak to me
Sometimes through me
Sometimes through others
He said it's in the darkness that faith sees best
Faith sees best in the darkness
I heard it
I heard you
I heard him
It landed because I know it to be true

It's in our darkest moments when our faith gets tested
When we rail against God
Doubt her/his existence
It's when anger or grief drains out our faith
It's in those dark moments that a light can go off
When it's easy to throw in the towel
It's when our faith gets tested that we find out if we have it
It's when we learn how to surrender let go give in
That our faith can take over

People talk about the power of their faith
They talk about how it strengthened them
How they lost it then got it back
I'm fascinated by that
Intrigued
. . .

So I ask many people questions about their faith
How did they get it
How have they sustained it
I ask because I know that I need to know
I ask because the people I admire most have a deep faith
It keeps them moving
They live in a place of love
It's where I want to live

I want to live in faith and not in darkness
Do I have to choose
I don't
I have faith

Those Moments

Life is endless moments
Like raindrops they pass through
Often unnoticed rarely counted

But then there are those moments when everything stops
Including your heart
Those moments are the ones you come back to over and over
    again
You look at those moments like little stones
You turn them upside down and right side up
You stare at them
Look for what you saw and what you missed
Those moments
You know what I'm talking about

The moment you left home and knew you weren't going back
The moment you saw that person you knew you would marry
The moment you gave birth for the first time
And held your child in your own arms
The moment your mother died and then your father
The moment you knew your marriage was over
The moment you knew you were leaving home again and not
    going back
The moment you knew your kids were no longer kids
And they didn't need you like you wanted to be needed
The moment you met your husband's new partner
That moment tears streamed down your face
You weren't trying to cry the tears just flowed

You knew you still loved him and always would
But you knew your moment was gone

That moment you realized there were more moments behind you
Than there would be in front of you
The moment you realized you had missed so many moments
That was the moment that hurt the most

Letting Go

The night before last I let go
I realized it was over
I was tired and done
Done trying to hold on
Done trying to be loved
Done trying to be important
Done trying
I surrendered to God
And when I did
I think I saw Jesus there in the corner curled up on the floor
Waiting to take me in
Waiting to hold me

The shaman talked me through
Over the hill he held on so I wasn't alone
I was so sad so hurt
I felt so abandoned so scared so desperate so alone
My arm was reaching out
It was instinct
I don't know why or how I did that but I was reaching out
Trying to hold on as they left
One by one
My mother left
My father left
Then him
He was the last to go and the hardest to let go of
After all I chose him
I chose him to rescue me

Never realizing that in truth I rescued me
I chose him to save me
Never realizing that I would have to save me
I chose him to protect me
But I had to learn that I would need to protect myself
He told me he was happy
He was free
With that I realized it was over
I needed to let go
And so I eased my grip released my hand and let go

I was and am alone
That wounded child crying out
Don't leave I'll do better
I'll do more
I'll try harder
No you won't

Let go
Let go
Let go
I loved you all in different ways
I know you loved me too in different ways
And so
I release you
You are free and finally so am I
I let go

I Didn't Know I Knew

Ever since I can remember
I was asking
Poking challenging pushing
Do you have this
The child asked
Are you the one
The one who is here to take care of me
Are you the one who will handle it for us
If not I'll find the one

The child searched the world
Poking pushing challenging grasping
The same questions over and over
Are you the one
Where is the one who will take care of me
Where is the one who can take care of the situation

Over hills up mountains and beyond
Always pushing always challenging
Searching running hoping
That someone anyone
Would take care of her
Hoping she could find the one

Then one day the man who says he's not a healer but simply a man
Spoke to the child now a grown woman
Can't you see he said that you have had it from the very
    beginning
You always were the one

The one who took care
The one who had it
You were always the one you were looking for
The one was in you
You had it and you have it
Rest breathe settle
You can stop looking
You can stop poking
You can stop pushing
Stop challenging
You are the one
You always were the one

Oh said the child
Ah said the woman

I didn't know she wept
I didn't know
But now I do

Accept What Is

You my imagination have carried me through
Through what was and what is with images of what could be
So strong are you that I live within your creations not within
     what is

I imagined a loving caring mother
I created her
Burying my longing shutting out my desire
My father I wanted him to be strong decisive in charge
My imagination landed on someone who was

Every man who has come by has been a figment of my
     imagination
My fantasy
I create people out of nothing
I attribute stories to them assign qualities to them
They become my creations
Until my creation clashes with what is

I created a world before meta before A.I.
I created my own universe and lived there
Because what was was unbearable unthinkable terrifying
     Unimaginable
And so I created what was livable
I existed in the imaginary
I disassociated to that place because I could survive there
With my made-up guards
My perfect husband
My loving attentive parents

My Sherpa my shaman
The strong-willed version of me
Until one day I let go of it all

At first I thought I was dying dissolving disappearing
But then I realized
My prayer for peace for connection for love for truth
Was being answered
For me to wake up the old must dissolve
Anxiety has to die so peace can show up
I must be stripped down to the basics

My ego is dying
But I'm waking up
My soul has melted me
I stepped out of the game into the light
I was alone
I looked around
I wanted to disassociate again but I didn't
I was OK
I was in the real world
Ready to live

I moved my wounds out of the way
So I could connect to you
The real you
The one who has been terrified to come out
The one who lives in the now

The Baseball Bat

The man handed me the bat
I stared down at the huge stuffed plastic bag in front of me
You have one hour he said
Then you will have another
Beat the shit out of this bag
Beat out every feeling every emotion
Get exhausted
Do it until you can't move
When you are done he said we will do it again tomorrow
And again and again
I can't I wailed

And then I did
With a fury I had never experienced
With a rage that would take out a mere mortal
No sooner had the bat come crashing down with such force
Did I realize how enraged how engulfed in anger I was

I killed that pillow and with it the darkness in me
I killed the criticism the gaslighting and the lying
I killed the unrequited love
I killed the weakness the excuse for manhood
All of it and then some
My rage took me aback and did me in

I lay there a heap of a woman a mess of a human exhausted
    undone
From killing the bag with my bat
That pillow was everyone and everything

I hit her I hit him I hit them and I hit me
I killed the dark in me
And I felt free
Lying on the floor everything that had been buried was out of me

The bat
I could have used you long ago
But like all things you came to me at the right moment
When I could lift you overhead and swing you with a power
I had never known

When I was done
I lay down the bat and that was that

Healed

The man said
My sense is that you are still broken
Living with sadness and despair
My sense is you haven't triumphed
You are simply trying to get there

Aren't we all just trying to get by I said
Trying to hang on
Trying our very best
Healed to me might not look happy to you

But the truth of life as it's unveiled itself to me
Is that some days one is grateful joyful triumphant
Other days one is lonely or sad
Unclear about the path ahead

Some people walk through life always looking
Joyful content at peace happy
Others of us navigate a different no less valuable road

Life has brought healing and happiness
Life has brought trouble and tragedy
Going through it brings humility and gratitude
For where one finds oneself

I feel triumphant said I to the man
Not on every day but on most
Healing looks like that he said

One step backward one forward
One breath at a time one smile at a time

Life is a marathon indeed
I've run I've crawled I've walked I've jumped for joy
I am what healing looks like
I have been healed by words that have touched my heart
Music that's torn down my walls
I've been healed by the wind and the rain
The plants and the flowers
I've crawled thinking I'd never walk again and yet
Hands broke through the clouds and pulled me up
Voices shouted stand up carry on continue

That's what triumph feels like said the woman
Healed is being here
Standing here
Loving all who passed thru
Loving those who stayed
Loving me loving you

Healed
Damn straight I am

Loving

The Dwelling Place

I dwell in possibility
Wrote Emily Dickinson
Where do you dwell she queried
In what do you dwell
Think about it

My heart pounded
I strained to think
Harder and harder
I searched for my dwelling place
My mind bounced
Not here not there
This question spoke to me from my deepest depths
Until all went quiet

You dwell in love
Said a little voice
My child you dwell in the hope of love the possibility of love
The healing nature of it
You were born from love
Now you live from that deepest source
You my child dwell in love
So be it

Searching for Love

Each of us is born into someone's arms
And if we are lucky we'll die in someone's arms
Everything in between is a search for our common humanity
Our quest is rooted in love

Where are you on the search
Have you found arms to hold you
Have you found the love you are searching for
Imagine someone looking at you the way your mother did
When she first held you in her arms
Imagine someone looking at you the way you looked at your
    first love

Your imagination is your gateway to your reality
Look at yourself like you are a miracle
A divine gift to the universe
Gasp in awe at all that you are
Oh my God you are amazing
Let your eyes rest on your magnificence on your light
Can you see the light within you
Can you see the miracle of the Creation of you

Imagine yourself in your mother's arms
Imagine the joy in that room
Believe me when I tell you
You deserve to be held in someone's arms
For the simple beauty of you

Motherhood

I was terrified to mother
Sure I couldn't do it well
Sure I wouldn't fit the bill
Sure I wasn't soft enough
To nurture to hold to care

But then you came along and my world changed
I fell in love and finally felt at home
I found what I had been searching for all along

From that moment on
I was only mother
Mother here mother there
I loved its arc
And I embraced its demanding ways
As each child grew into someone new

One marveled at the moon
Another found beauty in a flower
One gazed endlessly at the universe and its stars
While another had fun playing with cars

Day by day I became the mother I hoped to be
As I watched each of you become who you were meant to be
My fears fell away and my confidence grew
And the joy I had been looking for
Was finally found within each one of you

You

Now that I know you
I can't imagine life without you
Without your love your friendship
Your companionship your support

In fact no one who knows you can imagine life without you
It's not just the way you smile
Or the way your laugh fills the room
It's not just the way you care
Although the way you care blows everyone away

You care with your whole being
You care for those you love
Care for those who need to be cared for
You care for those who don't even realize they need to be cared for
But once they have been cared for by you
They know care in its purest form

There are so many things about you that I love I admire I respect
And that I am so grateful for
I'm grateful for
Your strength
Your kindness
Your love
I admire the way you chart your own course
I respect the fierceness that lies within you and raises its head
On behalf of those you love

And I am so grateful and proud to be your mother
Proud of the way you walk through life
Head held high shoulders back
Proud of the way you embrace your femininity
Your softness and your strength
I marvel at the way you toss your hair walk your walk speak your
    mind
And it takes my breath away to see you allow yourself to be so loved
So adored so held up high by those who love you
It's a thing of beauty
It's an act of divine intervention and inspiration
To be so loved

And so my child as you embark on this great adventure
Never ever doubt your worth
Never ever question your value
Never ever lose sight of who you are or where you came from

You stand on the shoulders of strong brave women
On your mother's side and your father's
Women who climbed mountains
Women who endured all that life can and does throw our way
And yet they kept going
That's who they were
That's who you are too

So never ever question whether
You have what it takes to stay the course
You do
And never ever wonder whether or not you deserve to be
    loved like this
 Adored like this

Valued like this
You are
It's exactly what you deserve

You my child were born from love and you were born to be
    loved
Yes you were born to be loved exactly like this

Love
Mama

This Moment*

Revel in this moment
Let it sink into every pore of your body
Let it touch your heart
Close your eyes and sit with it
It's your life
Breathe it in
That's freedom you are inhaling
That's love you are feeling

Celebrate this moment
Where you stand
One foot in childhood one in adulthood
They are both you and you are them
Never let adulthood rob you of your childhood
Remember to laugh to play
You are a mischievous child of God

Keep your wonder hold on to your awe
Your child voice is your compass
Your true self
Take her with you on your journey
Keep her close
She is you and you are she
Sit with her love her let her guide you on your journey

Celebrate who you are
You are free
Feel it breathe it in
It's your life
Sit in the wonder of you

My daughter Katherine's 18th Birthday Poem

Just for You*

Today is the day
Your graduation is here
Can you feel the excitement can you feel the joy
Pause
Reflect
Take a moment to feel what you feel

It is here
It is now
I've thought about it for so long
And yet it always seemed so far away
Now just like that it is here
It is now
I shake my head
I say wow

Today is your graduation day
Your day to step forward into your life
Today is your day to celebrate who you are who you have
    become
A young woman of tremendous worth
A young woman of substance, of beauty, of big feelings
A young woman with an open heart full of love
I say wow

Today is your day
Can you feel my pride can you feel my joy
You have worked so hard to be who you are

You have struggled you have taken a shovel and dug and dug
    and dug
What did you find my love?
You found a beautiful woman with a full heart a contagious
    laugh
You found feelings that were true
You know what you feel you know who you are
You know what makes you happy you know what is real in you

What is real is that you are smart, beautiful, compassionate,
Fashionable, witty, and true
That's who you are
That is you
All I can say is wow to you

―――――

On this day, my wish is for you to celebrate all that you are
Take in what you feel
As you step forward be open to love
Be open to laughter be open to the new
Be open, my Beanie, to all that is you

Be not afraid of the bumps on the road
You are strong you are true
You will know what to do
All I can do is say wow look at you

Remember to trust what you feel trust what you know is right
You know who you are
So go out my baby girl and step into your life
It's waiting for you
Enjoy what's to come
Own it embrace it adore it live it

On this day this is my wish for you
That you will come to see what I see in you

This is your day
This is your life
Go out and live it
You are my baby girl
You are the wow of my life

*My daughter Christina's 18th Birthday Poem

Him*

Him, that's you
She said it, it's true
You are "him" and I am "her"
"She made me do it," he always says
"Made me play that sport, sign up for that thing"
He rolls his eyes, shakes his head
She is she, he is him

She laughs at him, he makes her smile
There is no one like him, no boy, no man
He is a prince, a gentle soul
He is him

He likes to call her "Maria" or "her" or "she"
She knows when it's him
When he walks in the door, when he hugs her tight
When he calls
She knows he is sweet and gentle and true
He is him, she is she

She is Mummy, he is Patrick
He is 18 and extraordinary
She loves him to the moon and back
And when he leaves she will miss him so
He is him and she is she
"M-dog" is who she is. "What's crackin'" is what he says

She is Mummy, he is Patrick
Eighteen years of fun, love and laughter
He is "him" and her love for him will never dim
Happy birthday from "Her" to "Him"

My son Patrick's 18th Birthday Poem

The Man*

You were The Man the moment you were born
Special and wise deep and caring
Funny and loving
That's who you were
The baby yes
But The Man

Every man was a child
But not every child becomes a man
Not every man unfolds
Not every man becomes who God intended
But here you are
On the brink of adulthood
Wise before your age
Young at heart
Old in experience
You are The Man
Know it
Believe it
Let it sink into your soul
The one that developed long before you were born

It was you I spoke to long before you were born
About my dreams for you my hopes for you
When you were born I knew that you were in fact being
    reborn
It's true you have been here before
Wild and wise

Not of this time
And yet perfect for this moment

Here you are at adulthood
You will go out into the world
You will grow you will unfold you will affect all you meet
With your laugh your love your mind your amazing spirit
You are The Man with the joy of a child
You are a child who has grown into The Man

What an honor it has been and is to watch you unfold
To watch you find your way
To watch you retain the joy of a child within the intelligence
    of a man

A man who has studied
A man who has seen and felt
A man who has gone from holding his tongue to speaking his
    thoughts
A man who sees what others don't
Who notices everything and everyone
Wise beyond your years
Loving beyond your years

I shake my head
Where did you come from
How did I get so blessed to be able to travel
On this path called Life with you
To watch you grow to learn from you to be better kinder
To see what I used to overlook
You have loved me forward
You have made me a better person
Opened my eyes and my heart

You have made me a better woman by being the son you are
The man you have become is a teacher a guide
I love you to the moon and back
To Pluto and beyond
I love you more
You are The Man
Happy Birthday, Christopher

Love,
Mummy

My son Christopher's 18th Birthday Poem

Baby Girl

You came into this world
When it needed you most
You came into my world
When I needed you most

The first time I laid eyes on you
Was a video your Daddy took
Your Mama was holding you
You were crying
She was crying
And I started sobbing too
Uncontrollably to be honest
At the sight of you
At the sight of my baby girl holding her baby girl
I replayed that little video over and over
As I couldn't believe what I was seeing
Couldn't believe my eyes

And when I held you for the first time
The room grew still
My life slowed down
I felt at peace
You, little girl
My little grand-girl
In my arms so quiet and at peace

I traveled back in time to the moment
I first held your Mama in my arms
I had been so afraid

But as soon as I held her
I knew life as I knew it would never be the same
And it was good
I was a Mama
I was her Mama

And now
I'm a Mama G
A Grandmama
With grand plans for us
With grand hopes for you
For you, little girl
And for my little girl
You both are changing my world
Thank God for little girls

I Can't Wait to Meet You

Ever since I heard you were coming
I've found myself thinking about you

Who will you be?
What will you be like?
What will you like?
Will you like me?
Will we get to spend time together
Building sandcastles
Looking for leprechauns and mermaids
Will we watch movies go for walks
Will you get to travel with me
Will I get to show you the world
Will I get to show you my world
I sure hope so

I just know we'll be friends
I'll bet we'll laugh a lot
I'll sneak you candy and cookies
And we'll play games
Maybe we'll even have our own language
Our own special looks and winks

I can't wait until you're here
I'll bet it will be love at first sight
I'm so ready
I'm so excited
I'm so glad you are coming
I can't wait to meet you

The Two of You!

Isn't life magical
The way it unfolds
For so long you are one
And alone
Certain nothing can be done
No final piece for your puzzle
Sure no one is the one

Life is uncertain with its twists and turns
You wonder and wonder
Will there ever be The One
Who gets who you are
Who gets what you do
Who cares for your woes
And laughs at your ways
Will there ever be the one
The one?

But just when you're quite certain
It won't happen for you
You pull up a chair and he does too
And all of a sudden
The clouds open up the sun shines through
And one plus one equals *two*

And when that happens
You each know for sure
That all of your worry
Was so premature

Now the future's not hazy
Life no longer feels crazy
Pieces of the puzzle just fall into place
And you wonder
What did I ever do without you in my space?

Now that you are two
There is so much to do
Not out in the world
But deep inside of you

———

Look out for each other
Be devoted and true
Marvel at what God has given to you
Yes to you and to you
To both of you
Because now you are not just you
You are one plus one
Which is two

What you have
Is so precious and rare yes indeed
You both are so gracious so loving so gentle and true
So be kind be compassionate
That never gets old
And as you go on together and the years do unfold
Remember everything you've been told
About love about life
About husband and wife

Stay open stay loving
Keep it fun keep it true

You have one another
One and one equals two
And remember
The truth is that nothing the world has to offer
Is better than you two

You each deserve all that life has given to you
Don't doubt it don't question it
Believe that it's true
It's a gift
It's a treasure made just for you

And as you grow older may you always remember
This moment this day
And all the people gathered here
Sending you two on your way
May you recall all of the love that's here just for you
And all of the love to support and guide you on through

You are blessed you are honored
You're so lucky it's true
So love one another
And know that we love you
You are proof of God's matchmaking
How glorious it is that one and one make a perfect two!

Someone

On the day of your birth you become
Someone
Someone to love
Someone to hold
Someone to care for
To nurture and guide

You inhabit a name and you go out
Out into the world out into the unknown
You search out there to become
Some one

Never realizing that all of the some you already have
All the one you already are
Isn't it so
The search for someone takes you so far away
Away from the someone you already are

Your life unfolds
It sparkles and marvels
It's high and it's low
That's just how it goes
At times you find yourself wondering
Where oh where did the someone go

Blessed be the ones
Who believe
Believe that if God made me
Then I must be

Someone
Blessed be they who found the someone
In the one who they pledge to today

So on this day the day of your wedding you become
Someone to belong to
Once again you are someone to love someone to hold
Someone to honor
May you know this time that there is no someone out there
No one but the someone standing here before you

In truth it is you who must first stand before you
In your glory and your shame
Only then can another see you
And accept you and love you
The reflection of that love may blind even you

But don't be afraid don't run don't hide
The running can stop
You have been discovered
Discovered to be
Someone of worth
Someone worth loving

You are blessed oh yes you are
To be given this shot
This chance to love
This moment is sacred not just to one but to all

You are someone yes you are
You wouldn't be standing here if you didn't believe
Believe in the union of marriage
The union of love

. . .

You wouldn't be standing here if you hadn't found someone
The Someone in you
The Someone in him
The Someone in her
You wouldn't be here in front of the many
You have found the Someone to love you
The Someone to honor you
The Someone to hold you
The Someone to listen to you

My prayer and my hope for you both is this
Now that you have found Someone
May you live as joyfully and as peacefully as Someone
     times two
That is my ultimate wish for you

May You Rest

Today may you find rest on this
The day of your birth
May you catch a glimpse into the beauty of your heart
The sparkle of your eyes
May the ease of your kind smile
Smile down on you and
May you feel your body slowly unwind

Today may you stop the harsh wind that beats at your door
May you silence the raging voice that pushes you on
Until you can't take one more step do one more thing
Climb one more mountain

Rest my love
Let the chaos subside
Let the healing light come in
Yes there is calm there is peace
There is a space where you are more than enough
A space and place where you can rest
It's just around the river's bend

You're tired my love from the years spent trying
Exhausted from not being seen
Caring too much then not at all
Trying to figure out how to manage it all

Rest beneath the canopy of the trees bowing down
To the light to the breeze to the curve of the river
Watch how the river twists and bends

Watch how it rages then dissipates
Rises up with a vengeance
Then rests as the sun dries its unruly self

The sun understands
As do the trees
That the river churns
Mad at being contained and misunderstood
Angry at the shores that failed to offer it safe harbor and
    protection

Today the river is calm
It is choosing to bend in a place of grace
Choosing to pursue rest in a slice of heaven

Today the sun's rays bring the river to life
It shines it sparkles
Its beauty elicits gasps of awe and wonder

The banks by the bend hold space
For the birds and the bees
Hold space for the flowers that grow wild and untamed
The shores are strong rock-solid
Undeterred when the water surges at an unruly pace

Rest says the sun
Rest say the trees
You are more than the river
Not as jagged as its rocks
Not as destructive as you seem

On this day of your birth
Rest my love

Let go
Let it be

When you do
You will see
What you need to see
You will feel what you long to feel
You will know you are the river
The sun and the trees
The flowers and the bees
You will know who you have longed to be
But first you must rest
And allow things to be

Hope

———

My Life

I'm struck by how I've designed my life
It's not what I imagined as a young girl
I imagined myself with lots of kids
But I never imagined myself alone
I imagined myself as a matriarch but never without a patriarch
I always imagined I would be different from what people expected
More of a hippie
More monastic ethereal sassy sensual high-spirited
With hair flowing and a wide-brimmed hat
Doing my own thing
Making it up as I go
I'm a writer a poet a seeker a curious ball of energy
Simple complex fun deep wise
I know a lot and yet I know nothing at all

I don't really fit into society as we know it nor do I care to
I walk to a different beat
I've always known that about me
There is no place I can arrive at
Because there is no place that exists for me
There is no place I can get to because that place does not exist

And so here I am in constant conversation with God and
    with Mary
And with me
In constant conversation with my heart and soul
I'm in a constant flow like a river
I'm flowing

There's no party I'm trying to get into no club I want to join
No company I want to be beholden to
I'm a free spirit

When I sit on the porch early in the morning
Late into the evening
Often with a tear streaming down my face
Ah yes I battle sadness despair and loneliness
I breathe fear
I exhale it out but it sneaks back in

I keep breathing going writing trying to stay one step ahead
I am a free spirit
I look forward
I have no idea who will stand beside me if anyone
I reassure myself it's OK

I'm OK if I don't fit in
I never have
I never will
And so on I go

Silence Solitude Aloneness

I've rediscovered solitude silence aloneness
At first I was terrified to be alone
But then realized I've been alone in many ways my whole life
This discovery startled me but then allowed me to settle in
To reclaim the parts of me I used to love
Nature mystic wild child
The girl who went to concerts lay in the grass drank cheap wine
Smoked pot danced by herself and laughed her head off
That girl who rode horses to feel strong and free
Who ran from her brothers
And shouted down all who tried to come close
Who ran from the nuns the priests God himself

Today that girl runs to them
That girl loves the smell of newly mown grass
The language of horses
The companionship of God
The laughter of children
Music poetry
The biographies of saints
The forgiving of sins

That girl is this woman
Older but younger than she ever could be
Free from expectation
Delivered from evil
With permission to be the girl who was me
Yet could never be

Do What You've Never Done

I wanted to do something I didn't do
What do you want to do that you didn't do
Think about it
It's true
We all have things we have wanted to do but . . .
But what
But why
Why didn't we do what we wanted to do

I'll tell you
You're scared
It's a ghost that keeps you in fear
That ghost terrifies you
So you don't do the one thing you need to do
To free yourself

Go and do what you haven't been able to do
Don't tell me about your success your laurels all that you've done
You haven't done what you need to do
What you were put on this earth to do

You wanted him to do what you couldn't do
You wanted him to provide what you couldn't do
He couldn't give you what you didn't give you
So go back to the beginning and do what you need to do

Love your own self girl
That's right
Take care of yourself nurture yourself cherish yourself

Be loyal to you
Belong to your own heart
Own it protect it trust it

Remember this
The world can't love you
But one person can
But only if you do what you've never done
Love yourself let love of another in
Do what you've been too scared to do

I'm Trying to Center Myself

I'm trying to find my center
My sense of calm
My sense of balance
I move things around in my home to center myself
To bring order to my mind and calm to my body
I try to clear clutter hoping it will calm my nerves

As I read through my journal
I realize that trying to find peace find calm and find love
Has been the huge pursuit of my life
Calm peace love centering
I've looked for these things these feelings everywhere
And in all the wrong ways

I'm a contemplative monastic soul
Love has been elusive to me
Calm has been elusive to me
Order has been elusive while chaos has swirled around me
I've spent my life trying to make my life make sense
Trying to find order so I could relax

Now that I realize this I can stop
Stop the doing stop the running and rushing stop the mania
Everything is in its place
Everything is how it's supposed to be and where it's supposed
    to be
Everything on the outside is in order
It's serene it's clean it's organized
Nothing left for me to do there

Now I can declutter and reorganize my insides
Where do I start

First I must be aware
I'm now clear that the order the peace I crave must start on the
    inside
I'm a good person
Do I believe that core truth
I shake my head no
Why wait?

Let me start at the beginning
I was created by God
Inside of me I am divine
So at my core in my center I am good I am divine
I am the work of God Almighty

I am Love
I was made to love and be loved
I was loved when I was born
And nothing was wrong with me when I was born

I'm going to make sense of my life.
I can because now I know that in my center in my core I'm good
I'm divine I'm worthy of being loved I know how to love
I know how to take care
In my core in my being I know there is nothing wrong with me
My needs are not too much
I am not too much

If Not Now When

The adventure known as life
Starts with an explosive entry
You spend decades wandering immune to the constraints of time
Until the urge of your soul
Your mystic calling
Overwhelms all else
Your separateness which has been at the root
Cries from deep within
You know you have come to the end of this part of your adventure

Poet prophet writer mystic
Delve deep ask from where does this calling emanate
From where does this separateness speak
You dip your toe in then recoil
Covered in fear in shame you retreat
The voice speaks if not now when

It's getting late you are burnt
You are out
You are dwelling in an empty well
If not now when

Take off your cloak of restlessness
Take off your cloak of shame
You are more Magdalene than Mary
More wind than Mariah
More St. Francis than St. Clare
More monastic than social
Fall into the you you've run from
If not now when

Stop the Doing

Stop the Doing the man says
It's the Doing that's killing you

The Doing
The Doing has been in my life
The Doing is me
I am the Doing
If I stop do I cease to be

Stop the Doing the man says
The Doing you do to you
The mind that judges
The mind that critiques
Stop that Doing
Then you will heal
Then you will nurture
Then you can cure
Stop that voice
Stop the doing

Lie Down

When you lie down and close your eyes
What are the memories that roll through
Do you know
Close your eyes
See what rolls through
Are they tragic joyful disturbing shaming
Lie back here they come
Rapid at the start

Giving birth
The aftermath
Holding your child for the first time tight to your chest
Exhausted but exhilarated
My daughter sleeping

In no particular order they come
I see myself getting married
Pre-school and yes way too many funerals
Holding a book I wrote in my hands
Holding a book in my hands that moved my heart
Staring into someone's eyes
Someone I loved and someone I barely knew
My granddaughter smiling at me
Laughter with friends
Staring at myself gasping at my youthful beauty and now my
    worn face
I smile back at me

My parents looking down at me from heaven
Me getting an award for my advocacy my mothering my being

This life what a ride it's been
I wouldn't trade it for the world none of it
Well maybe some of it

But oh what a ride it's been
You orchestrated it all from a place deep within
You are the conductor
Life is your orchestra

Regrets

I used to say I had none
Everything happens for a reason
Everything provides a lesson
So I carried on.
No regrets only lessons
Said she
I'd do it all again exactly the same

Really?
Would I really want that pain again
Would I really try to climb that mountain again
If I knew the top wouldn't be what I thought?
Knowing what I know now
Would I really do it all exactly the same?
Absolutely not

I'd speak up more not for others but for me
I'd be gentler kinder more patient
I'd stop abusing my heart my mind my body
I'd stop and rest
I'd act more like love
I'd be so different.
Regrets you betcha.
Lots of them
But.

Go Find What You Need

You my love are still looking
Looking for what you need
Looking for what you think will make you feel enough
Feel big
Feel good
Feel loved
I want you to be happy
I want you to be free
I want you to know you owe nothing to me

Go run
Go play
Go be free
You haven't found what you need in me
We all look to another to fill that hole
Created long ago by another not me
But that's yours to figure out
Yours to see through
It's your home to build
Just not with me

So wave goodbye to my heart
Let it sail off to sea
You owe nothing to it or to me
I thought you were solid and know you did too
But sometimes love just can't get through
Go find what you need
Go find what you want
Go look for what's missing
I pray it fills your heart

How Did We End Up Here

She walked across the room
It seemed like she moved in slow motion
But it was slow motion getting here
Years of waiting
Years of anguish
Years of tears
Years of not knowing
All gone in an instant
As she walked across the room years fell away
Her eyes held his gaze as if no one else were in the room
No one else in the world
He stood dark jacket white shirt black slacks black shoes,
    boots in fact
A black belt with a silver buckle cuff links that sparkled
Her eyes caught the watch on his wrist
His looks took her breath away and still she kept walking
    right to him
She'd been walking to him her whole life
But somehow could never get there
Every time she thought she was almost there the table moved
But this time was different
His eyes never moved from hers
They filled with tears
He held out his hand took hers and kissed it gently
I've been waiting for you he said I'm sorry it took so long
Me too she said

But we are here and it doesn't matter how we ended up here
It just matters that we ended up here

They talked they laughed they reminisced they dreamed ahead
And then he stood up and said I'm sorry but I'm leaving I can't
    stay
I just can't
She nodded said she understood
Even though nothing could have been further from the truth
Her eyes locked with his
No one else was in the room all was quiet
Just like that he was gone

She sat at the table
The candle burned
The music filling the room slowly faded away
She sat she blinked back tears
Stared out and said aloud to the empty room
How did I end up here?
And a voice from deep inside said
You ended up here because
That's exactly where you were meant to be
She nodded closed her eyes and died

Being Alone

Being alone has brought me to my knees
Being alone has brought me face to face with the depths of my soul
Brought me face to face with my own longing
The depth of my longing
The depth of my desire
Being alone has brought me face to face
With my light and my darkest crevices
With my tenderness and my raging anger and relentless drive
Being alone has allowed me to truly know myself
Understand myself and finally to have compassion for myself

Learning compassion for myself has given that self in me
    strength
It's given the self in me a resolve I never had before
Because it's made me realize how kind I am
How loving I am
How good I am
It's made me realize that I deserve someone like this
Because I'm not that bad mean person
I thought I was that person who deserved to be mistreated
I am this self I now know I am

One by One

One by one she gently brought them to the circle
Each sat unaware that the one right next to them was them
One by one they came until the circle was round and full
The two-year-old
The five-year-old
The eight-year-old
The twelve-year old
The thirteen-year-old
The fifteen-year-old
The forty-five-year-old
The fifty-year-old
And the fifty-five-year-old
They had been brought together for a reason.
She looked into the eyes of each one and assured her
That all was okay

She made her way around the circle
She gently showed them their older selves
Each age had been ruptured by trauma
Each age was stuck in her own place of terror
Never having been held comforted or soothed
The mother took each part of herself
Calmed the child within
Brought her into her being

This woman in the last part of her life
Knew this ceremony was critical to her own healing
She could not heal until she had healed

All the splintered parts of herself
This woman could not heal until she had gone back
Picked up each version of herself
And brought her to safety
It was the work of a loving gentle strong nurturing mother

To be whole requires you to leave no part of yourself behind
To be whole requires you to heal the parts of yourself
That have been frozen in trauma
Frozen in terror
Frozen

————

Go back
Pick up the pieces of you
Bring them to a place that is safe
With the light from God allow them
To thaw
To heal
To see
To know

Bring them home
Then you are home

It's Saturday Night

The house is quiet except for the rain
There is so much rain
So rare for here
This much rain this hard
I sit up in my bed and listen
For minutes I listen to the tapping the wind the swish
And I'm surprised that I feel this overwhelming sense of happiness
I turn my head as if happiness were a guest coming into my home
Look at you here
You like the rain
You like the quiet
You like sitting here in the rain in front of the fire all by yourself
I surprise myself
I smile and I go back to listening to the gift of the rain

Home

———

There Will Be That Moment

There will be that moment
When you notice yourself dazzling
You will be amazed
You will feel it
In the places of your skin that used to house your pain
That you used to write about
You will step back in awe and in recognition
Of all that brought you to this moment
Turned out it was gradual it had to be
You thought it was painstakingly slow
Now you see now you feel
You couldn't have stood here and felt it any sooner than this
    moment
It would have blinded you
You wouldn't have believed it
Or trusted it
Now with amazement you see
Dazzling is for those who stay the course
Dazzling is for those who risk losing everything
To see with new eyes
To feel with an open heart
Who knew
Dazzling is for the fearless

Making Room for Me

I've started making room
At first I didn't know what I was feeling
Everywhere I looked I saw too much
Too many books too many pictures too much of everything
I pushed my arms out
Move away
Get away I said
I did the breaststroke
Pushing out
I need space I thought
I need room
Room to breathe
Room to see
Room to settle

I started clearing out
The clutter
The mess
The old
I looked out
Out at nature
Out at space

In the dawn of morning
It dawned on me as I meditated
That what I was craving
What I was doing
What I was preparing for was

Making room for me
Not a room but room

I am after all at the end of an era
Much of my work in the home is done
So it's logical I need to make room for this next moment
What it will be I don't know
Where will it take me I don't know
Will I walk alone
Will I lead
Will I follow?

I'm making room to know
I'm making room for me
To step in step up step out
I'm making room for something new
I don't know
Do you?
All I know is that I need to make room

Time Is Passing By

The days and nights go rolling by
Time is a-wasting
It's been a while since I heard your voice
Even longer since I saw your eyes
I can't remember how your hand felt in mine or your body next
    to mine
I can't remember why you liked me or if you ever did
Perhaps it was all a cloud a mirage something that just blew past
But wait I do remember the stories you told me
They are fading but I can remember how I felt when you told
    them
I felt full
I felt happy
I felt peace
I felt at home
I guess I remember what's important
It's that home is deep inside me

Mama G

Look at me now
I said to myself in the mirror

It has taken me years to not recoil from the face staring back at me
To not look at her and feel overwhelming pity
To not judge her harshly for allowing such destruction to occur on
   her watch
To not feel anything but judgment towards her

Now finally I look at her with compassion
I look at her with reverence and joy
She, as in me, is in her prime
Loving the life she has created

Today that woman revels in the now
Mama G, I am
Mama G

Today I play with my grandchildren on the same playgrounds I
   took my babies to
I play the same games of hide and go seek I taught my children
I read *Goodnight Moon* and *Love You Forever* and I still cry like
   a baby

I marvel at the now adults I birthed into this world
Look at them, I say, over and over
They blow me away

I'm humbled by all they've been through and yet how tall they
   stand

How united they are
I'm grateful for my presence in their lives

Lucky me, I say to that woman staring back at me
Lucky you lucky you lucky you
You are alive and you are still playing
You are still laughing and you are still loving
Look at you, Mama G

There is so much life in you
So much life ahead of you
You have yet to write the end of your story
I, for one, can't wait to see how it all unfolds

No matter where you are on your journey, stay the course and
    keep climbing
The view will be worth it

Do not stop until you look in the mirror and marvel
At the person staring back at you
Mama G

Lucky you
Lucky me
Lucky us

Hand It Over to God

I'm handing myself over to God
It's a relief to do it
Ever since I was young I felt this pull to God
But I resisted it
I'd read the biographies of saints
Of those who had handed their lives over
And they all died young in brutal ways
So I ran
Ran away from knowing I was being called
I wasn't going to die at the stake
I wasn't going to be a saint
And so I ran

Then I found myself depending on my faith in God
I found what I had run from slowly resurfacing
There you are I said knowingly
I will no longer run from you
I am called
I've always been called
I tried on the Devil tried on the hustle the climb
I always kept coming back to you

My Father who art in heaven
I wouldn't be who I am today without your love
Your guidance
Your support
Our Father
Hallowed be thy name
I succumb

I Wish

I wish you peace
I wish you joy
I wish for you to be gentle with yourself

Take away the rules
Take away the judgments
Take away the hardships
Take away all the tests you put your mind and body through
I know you can survive on little to nothing but why
Ask yourself why

Why should you starve
Why should you do and be without
Why does everything have to be so stark
Ask yourself why
Then ask yourself why not

Why should you not be enveloped in love in kindness
Why should you not be easy on you and ask others to be as well
Why should you not be surrounded by beauty
Why should you not
I think when you ask yourself why should you not
You will find out why you should

Away with Me

Do you want to go away with me
To a place with a view
To a place we haven't been
Just you and me
Alone
We can walk when we want
Be when we want
Do what we want
Imagine just you and me

Are you afraid
That you are not enough
Are you afraid of what might come up
I sense your fear
Your deep unrest
I sense you feel you cannot go
But I'm calling you
Calling you to go away with me

I sense you will be more than fine
You will walk with me
Talk with me
Lie down with me
You will rest
You will dream

Come away with me
To a place where you will see
See what I've always seen

That you are enough
Enough for me
I am you
I'm calling you
To come away with me
Me and you
We are one

Come away
Walk with me
Talk to me
Rest with me
Lie down with me
We are one
Will you come?

I'm the Defender Now

I'm the defender now
The defender of me

My story
I left my marriage
I rebuilt my life my home my center my core
I built a safe space a healing space
I've rebuilt my circle
My life may look smaller on the outside
But it's calmer on the inside

I'm a good person
I take responsibility for myself
I know I can be restless and exhausting
I know I ask a lot of questions
But I also know I'm a lot of fun
I have a monastic soul
I'm an introvert and an extrovert
I've misread situations but I can right them too

I'm the defender of the little girl who felt she had no one
That was sad but it's made me strong

I'm going to defend myself protect myself honor myself
I am an original I am a lot
I'm a warrior like Minerva
Damn right I am

Life Is Hard and Then It's Not

Life is hard and then it's not
It's frenetic and busy
Then one day you wake up
And it's quiet and you are alone

No one tells you that one day
You can just be sitting there
And a note from a friend can make you burst into tears
Just because it's kind
Just because it touched a piece of your heart

No one tells you that you will spend years berating yourself
Only to realize one day that you didn't need to
You didn't need to run around like you did
Play the games that you did
You didn't need to be so tough
It was all such a waste of your time
Your precious time

No one tells you
It will be about the little things
They tell you it's the big things
It's not

It's about when a child grabs your hand
It's about the way someone looks at you
It's about a hug a note a song
It's about all the things they don't tell you about
That's why I'm telling you

Gratitude

I want to thank you for all you have done for me
I found myself through your words
I realized how I wanted to be treated through your actions
And I realized my worth by letting it all into my heart

When I look in the mirror I see who you saw
I see a good beautiful soulful woman
One who loves
One who laughs
One who creates
One who loves beauty
One who loves to be wooed and charmed
One who loves to work and create and relax and think

I thank you for the lessons and your patience
I'm sorry I can't stay
I must go
I'm sorry I can't take you with me
I'm sorry I can't take care of you
I'm sorry I can't be what or who you need

I know you will find who and what you're looking for
Not in your fantasies or your dreams but here on earth
Someone who can accept you just the way you are
Someone who has the same wants and dreams
Someone who won't try to change the way you dress
Or the place you live
Or the things you say and do
Someone who loves you as is

I wanted to be that person but it turns out I'm not
I know you know that I can feel it
I know you do too
May we part as we met
Two wanderers along the broken road
Until we meet again

Keep Coming

When you stop becoming you stop the creation of you
When you stop unfolding you stop the beauty of you
Keep coming keep coming
Step out into the light
Step up to the top of the mountain
Speak up from that place
Stay strong stay the course in your own becoming
Stay the course in your own unfolding
Be not afraid
What you should fear is that you don't become
Who you were meant to be

Unfold and keep coming said the voice inside of me
Keep coming
I said no I want to rest
I want to go home
The more I struggled to resist the harder it became
Keep coming she said
Keep unfolding
Give birth to yourself
Let her in let her out
She is in there

You have permission to be yourself
Keep coming keep unfolding rise up
You have permission to be you

It is all I have ever wanted for you
It is all God has ever dreamed of for you
Keep coming
Be not afraid
Keep coming

Looking Back

It's early morning
The birds seem to have lost their minds
It makes me think
Of the time when I lost mine
Every morning my mind felt cluttered confused scattered
    hopeless
I couldn't see my way forward
The ground below me felt like quicksand
My breath was shallow
Panic was my everyday companion

This morning I'm amazed I no longer feel that way
The ground underneath me is solid
My wings feel like my own
I love my quiet time
My aloneness
My life

I've surprised myself
How did I get here
I can only say day by day
By not giving up
By staying in the grind
By pursuing the Open Field
I believed it existed
And so it does

Inside of me and everywhere I look
I wish someone had told me
But of course they did
But I had to learn it myself to believe it
And so I did

On the Mountaintop

I climbed up here the moment I came home
Home from dropping my last child off at college
Climbed up here to prove to myself that I could
I came up here to look at the ocean
To feel the wind whip at my face

I came up here to cry
To breathe
To be
To reflect back
To dig down and find my hope for the future

I sit on the bench named after my friend and look out
Out into the vastness of the world
We are all such tiny drops
And yet we spend our lives performing struggling
Trying to get the big world to notice
It doesn't care

I see a little sailboat off in the distance
It bobs out there alone
A big boat with beautiful majestic sails comes close
And then turns its beautiful self away and off it goes

Life can do that too and yet you have to keep sailing
With the wind and against the wind
Sometimes you bob
Sometimes you sit up on the mountain like I do today

Looking out
Taking it all in

I take a deep breath
I feel compassion for that little boat bobbing
And compassion for the little girl inside of me
I have compassion for the big majestic boat too
Being majestic looking majestic
Sailing with your sails full all the time is a lot of pressure
I can see them both from my perch on the mountain

I wasted so much time and energy all my life trying to fill my sails
I can see that now
I'm sorry I did that to me
I thought if I could only get to the mountaintop
Everything would be different

I'm here now
Alone
It's all different
But not in the way I dreamed
You have to climb up here to know what I mean

I Sat on My Porch

I sat on my porch
It was dawn
As I do every morning
I recited my gratitude list and watched the light break through the
    trees
The fire crackled
I looked up and out
Then I felt it
At first I wasn't sure what it was
Then it slowly made its way down my cheek
And I knew
It was a tear
I touched my cheek
It was damp
My eye was wet
Life is like that

I'm Over You

On an unsuspecting morning
I looked up at my tree
At the birds soaring by and the wind blowing by
I felt a certain something
A smile crossed my face
Tears welled in my eyes
A lightness came over me
My eyes
I could feel them laughing
My eyes were laughing for all to see
What a concept what a thrill
I realized then and there
There and then
I was over you

Through God's Eyes

I admit I didn't always see the world the way I see it today
I didn't always see myself the way I do today
For much of my life the world was black and white
Right and wrong
I judged myself harshly and pushed myself relentlessly
But along the way my vision shifted
I came to realize that beating myself up didn't ultimately serve me
Running myself into the ground only exhausted me
And seeing the world the way I was seeing it
Was narrow and shortsighted
I started to see myself and the world with a gentler gaze
And one day I realized I was seeing myself through God's eyes

I Live with Two Dogs

I live with two dogs
Yes I do
And remarkably neither one of them is really mine
Champ belongs to my youngest
Maverick belongs to my eldest
But they live with me
How this came to be
Is beyond me
But it really no longer matters
What matters is
I live with two dogs
They are my roommates
They play they tussle they rumble they cuddle
They are needier than any one of my kids ever was
One bites one barks
But both respond to love
So I give it
Freely daily always

I live with two dogs
I never thought this would come to be but it has
I share this because you too may end up
Living with two roommates
Who don't look like you act like you talk like you
But those roommates

Might have a love language just like yours
Isn't life funny

I live with two dogs
We are three
Champ Maverick and Me

Born

It happened almost 60 years to the day
It was a Sunday
The strangers walked in
Into her space
They held it these strangers all five
Yes they did

Up first was the elder
She beckoned you back
Back to your youth
She urged you and she pushed you to make peace with the past

Pick up the child she said in a whisper
Tell her she's safe
Tell her you love her and that you'll take her out of that place
The place where she's scared alone in the room
Tell her you'll carry her safely away
Away from her fears
Away from that room

I lay on the bed
Too tired to move
Not really wanting to rescue the child in that room
Know this said the elder wise with her words
You can choose to calm to comfort to love or you can walk away
But know if you do
That child in you will torment you and run you
And cause you continued pain
She will frazzle your brain
Cause havoc in your heart
And keep you split into many different parts

. . .

The man who was the healer stepped forward to see
To see if he could tame the child within me
He spoke in a whisper
His eyes looked straight through
Don't you know
Don't you know all the love that's here for you
With grace and with mercy his voice just got through
The tears came tumbling out like rain on the ground
The strangers stepped forward and wrapped her with love
    all around

She wailed and she cried because she finally felt
Felt she was loved
Loved by God
Loved by strangers
Loved by all in the room
Loved by the woman who was born again in that very room
That woman bent over picked up the child in the room
And carried her safely to her womb

The walls they tumbled
That morning they did
The pain fell away like morning dew
In its place was love
Mercy hope and you
You were reborn
On that Sunday
Thank God that's true

Reborn

I used to scoff at the idea
That someone could be reborn
Please
So skeptical was I
I would smile
Pretend to care
But I knew that you couldn't be reborn
Please

But then
There I was
Dark and forlorn
With walls all around
And it happened
I was reborn
Put away your doubt
Put away your scorn
Don't roll your eyes
Believe me when I say
I was reborn

I came through into the light
Into the love
I cried
Gasped for air
I was held
I was soothed

I knew that God was in the room
I was wrapped in love
I was held with care
I was safe
I was here
I was there
I was healed
I was held
I was love
I was born
Into the light
Into love
Into life
I am reborn

My Tree

There is a tree I look at every morning
It stands in my backyard
Most days I just look at it
I see nothing
I feel nothing
It's just a tree

But today was different
Today I noticed
Its grace
The space between its branches
The way it almost touches the sky
The way it holds the little lanterns as the wind knocks them
    around
Today I noticed the buds on its bare branches
It showed me it's alive
I saw that today
I saw

It's coming back through all the years I've been looking at this tree
I never noticed this
That this tree always stands tall
Always offers shade
Always offers a place to sit under its vast umbrella
It offers light
It holds a place for the lanterns
It's there every morning
Strong stable solid

Standing holding its place
Embracing all that there is
Nothing has killed it
Nothing has knocked it over
It's alive
It's about to bloom
It's emerging
Today when I look at the tree
I see myself like I see the tree
And that revelation makes me smile

My New Name

I love being a Mama G
What's that, say you to me?

A Mama G is a grandma, a goat of a mom
She's the one who paved the way
Until her kids were done

She's the one who now steps forth and says
Go run! Go play!
Give them to me go have a day!

Mama G may be a whole new name
But the games can be the same
The laughter the walks and talks
The hide and go seek

Who knew it would reignite the child in me?
Who knew that the memories would come flooding back in?
Who knew I could remember the songs the way they used
    to be

Loving never gets old and neither does play
Being a mama G is a role I love
I'm so grateful to have a chance to laugh and learn and
    love again
Being a Mama G makes life complete
And when I hear my name
I don't skip a beat

I Met Someone

I met someone
And guess what?
It's me!
I've come to know what I never knew about me
I'm lovable and beautiful and I'm a survivor
I survived neglect and betrayal
I survived heartbreak and loss

Today this is what I know
I know I am lovable hooray!
I am also loving and beautiful
And kind and caring and thoughtful and nurturing and
    tenderhearted
I am worthy and I am a divine creation of God
I am a dreamer an artist a creator a protector
I'm brave really really brave
I am strong and I am a survivor and I can make French press
    coffee
I can make tea
I can love you without losing me

I can drive a car
Sail a boat
Ski down a mountain and climb back up if I need to
I can make a beautiful home
I can raise great kids
I can dress up or dress down
I can read a book and write one too

I can watch a movie and produce one too
There is much I cannot do of course but why linger on those
　　things
I'm finally focused on all that I can do all that I am all that I bring
And all that is unique to me
You see I'm a survivor and that's been no easy feat

So take it from me
I'm allowing what is to be a triumph not what isn't
Let the others do that
As for me
I'm just going to look up at the sun the moon and the stars
And give thanks
I'm glad to be me

I Finally See You

I finally see you
Not him
Not her
Not them
The mirror once so crowded is finally clear
I see you

You did everything for them to see you
For them to take note of who you were
Never stopping to see who you are
Now it no longer matters
It no longer matters whether they see you

Wipe away the fog on the mirror
You are free
On this day look at what you see
On this morning
Know that you are seen
By the only one worth seeing you
Good morning Maria

Marvel

Life is a marvel
Yet we seldom stop to do that
Marvel at what we have
Marvel marvel marvel
Not just at what you have endured sustained created
But at who you are
Marvel at the way you smile
At the way your eyes shine
At the way you make others feel when you look at them
Marvel at your strength
Marvel at your calm
Marvel at the way you see the world
Open beautiful good
It's the way you are too
Marvel
I know
I do

Happily Alive

Here I sit in my happily ever after phase
The bow is not wrapped around a couple
It's wrapped around me

My love source is everywhere
My adult children, their partners
My grandchildren
The squeals of delight when they see me fill me up
My extended family and friends
My God, they are my source my happily ever after

So many need an updated image of happily ever after
An updated story line
One where one can stand at the center glowing and beaming
Fully alive and letting love in from multiple sources

This is a new story
I get love from you
I get love from my community
I get it from my work and from the stranger in the coffee line

There may not be a special someone, but that doesn't make me
    less special
Or less of a someone

I stand in this new chapter
Bursting forth with life with love
My mission and my feet are firmly planted on the ground

. . .

I look up to my God and I look around at nature
I close my eyes and give thanks to all who loved me and those
   yet to be
I say I'm happily alive
It doesn't always take two
It just takes me

Blessed

Blessed
Every day I tell myself I'm blessed
Blessed by God
Blessed by grace
Blessed by love
My life hasn't unfolded exactly as I imagined
I bet you feel the same
My life has more jagged edges and unpleasantries
Than I care to admit
I bet the same goes for you
Yet I know when I sit looking at my tree
I am blessed

Not everyone gets to my age
Not everyone knows the love I've known
And not everyone knows the heartbreak I've felt
But still I know I'm blessed
Maybe not in ways I imagined
But in ways that I can feel

I'm blessed by the sun on my face
I'm blessed by the presence of my children at my table
I'm blessed by a few good friends who tell me
I'm a blessing in their lives

I didn't always believe I was a blessing
Far from it
I wore a cloak of being too much

Too exhausting too talkative too relentless too everything
I wore the cloak of shame that comes from feeling ashamed

But today
On this fine summer day
I know I am blessed
I know it because I've decided it's true
I've decided and perhaps you will too
To be a blessing
I smile at the thought
I smile at the truth
As should you
Like you I'm blessed by God
Blessed by grace
Blessed by love
Blessed by you

On Earth as It Is in Heaven

For years I tried connecting to her
To you on the other side
Nothing
No matter how hard I tried
No matter how many times
I came up
Empty

I wanted to know what you thought
I needed to know whether you approved of my path
I felt desperate to connect
. The hole you left on earth left in my heart
Was like a crater
And so I searched for signs
I asked around
Nothing

Until something
From heaven as it is on earth
Connecting with my mother on the other side made me weep
It brought me joy it brought me peace
It was as if
As if she were here
She said she was happy
Free of pain and that she and my father were having
"The spiritual time of our lives"
Amen
. . .

It wasn't on earth as it was in heaven
It was different up there
She was different
Still strong still funny still her
But now she had something she didn't have on earth
Softness gentleness happiness
She had freedom
Freedom to be her most authentic self

She apologized for being so tough so demanding so hard
She didn't know another way
I believed her I knew that to be true
I forgave her I told her I loved her
And this time she didn't push me or pull away
On earth as it is not in heaven

She went on
She was proud of me said I was on the right track
She said she loved me
Connecting to her in heaven brought relief to me on earth.

Hail Mary Mother of God
Pray for us sinners now until the hour of our rebirth amen
What is in heaven can be felt on earth
In the name of the mother the daughter and the Holy Spirit
Amen

The Long Road

I took the long road
The long road from me to me
I had the whole world
But I didn't have me
Jesus warned us about that
But there were so many distractions along the way
So many bright lights
So many smart people I thought were wiser than me
Yes I took the long road from me to me

I didn't know
That if I didn't know me
Then I couldn't help you
And we couldn't become a we
I went from we to you
And forgot about me

I gave you me but I sold me cheap
I didn't negotiate I didn't believe
Didn't believe that it stopped and started with me
Yes it was about you
I never believed in me

I took the long road
It brought me back to me
It's a long road but it ended where it should
It ended with me

Never Too Late

I stand here in this next chapter
In this stage of life fully embodied
Fully engaged

I never imagined myself in this place
My dreams my visions
As a young girl I pictured me differently
I thought I'd feel done
How wrong was I

In so many ways I feel like I'm just beginning
In so many ways all that's been done all that I've been through
has brought me to this unimagined place

I never honored my creativity my innovative spirit my ability to
    reinvent reignite look ahead and beyond
I do now

I didn't plan where I stand today
I simply kept asking kept prodding
I allowed my curiosity to lead me into the unknown
Down uncharted paths
Into dark forests through swamps into mud
I allowed my inquisitive nature to push me forward into realms
    I had never fathomed
Into unimagined places I felt I had no business being
And yet there I was exactly where I was meant to be

Creating companies and publishing books
Producing films and creating federal initiatives

All while playing on swings building sandcastles playing hide and
    go seek with my grandkids

My heels took me from the principal's office to the Oval Office
From the anchor desk to the kitchen table
From one political party to a new one yet to be imagined

My uncharted life—my unimagined life—is authentically my own
At this very moment, I look back, I look ahead and I see only
    possibilities for you and for me

It's never too late to live the life you imagined
And it's never too late to live a life you never imagined
So live the life that's meant exactly for you

Freedom

I stood with eyes closed
My arms outstretched palms facing up
I looked up towards the heavens
I took in a deep breath and allowed this new feeling
To make its way through my body into my heart
Up to my throat my eyes
I could feel the tears streaming down my face

There in my mind's eye
I saw my parents
An angel standing between them holding their hands
There was light all around them
They all gazed down at me
And I felt enveloped in love
My breathing picked up speed
I was now crying uncontrollably
My eyes were still closed my arms still thrust out
I felt like I was bathed in light
And in that moment I felt free
My heart was full
My mind totally quiet
I was amazed by myself
I had scaled my own mountain

I stood there clear for the first time
For the first time in my life I felt
There was absolutely nothing broken about me
Nothing wrong with me

I was not too much nor was I not enough
None of what I had thought about me was true
None of what I had been led to believe was so
I was and am a light
I knew then and there
I am love and I am lovable
I was home I was free
And I could barely contain the love I felt for me

It's true
There is light beyond the darkness
There is clarity beyond and below the confusion
I could feel the strength in my body
My legs held me up as I gazed up towards the light and it
    covered me
I never gave up searching I never gave up trying I never gave in

I put my hands over my heart bowed my head and whispered
Thy will be done
On earth as it is in heaven
You are free Maria
All of that was then
This is you now
You made it home to yourself I'm so proud you
My child blessed are you

Welcome home
Hallelujah
Amen

My Morning Meditation

I just finished my morning meditation
And this came to me
Perhaps for the first time
I like me
I like my life
I'm proud of me and the journey I embarked on
The strength I've had to make it through

I'm happy sitting here on my porch with Champ
The candles are lit the fire is on
It's quiet
Quiet in my home and quiet in me
That makes me smile

My morning meditation brought me to this place of realization
I'm alone but I'm OK
I'm kinder than I used to be
Gentler than I used to be
Less scared than I used to be
Less angry
I like the energy in my home
And I like the energy in me
I've tapped into my femininity and my masculinity
But today I spend more time in my femininity
That's good
I'm good

Sure things scare me like being alone for the rest of my life
But if that's what happens so be it

I will continue to surround myself with beauty
So I can access the beauty the spiritual the feminine in me

I like me
Look at that
I smile
Welcome Maria
Welcome home

I See the Light

I see the light
It breaks through
First with a sliver
Then a burst
Flooding all that there is
Light
I raise my face to it
Close my eyes
And bask

The light grows
Into my heart
Up through my chest
To my mind
I don't recognize it at first
But then slowly a smile crosses my face
Unknowingly unwittingly I feel the light
There is hope
I am good
Say goodbye to the dark
Hello to the light
It bursts forth from within
Finally I see and feel the light
I made it
Amen

And So . . .

I am Maria
I was raised in chaos in a very famous family
My mother wore pants and worked all the time
She was always in a rush
And she was often sick and distracted
But despite all that
She changed the world
With her drive and her fierce determination

My father was a handsome, gentle man
He lived for my mother
I wanted him to be tougher and stronger
But I didn't realize his strength was internal
And he changed the world in his ways too
With his imagination, his intelligence, his faith in God, and in
    others

When I was five my uncle became President of the United States
I moved with my parents and two brothers to Washington, DC
We lived in a hotel
When I was eight in third grade
I was sent home from school and wasn't told why
No one was home when I got there
My parents were gone
Just my brother Bobby and I were there
I guess Timmy was too since he was a baby
I have no recollection of anyone talking to me that day
It was all because my uncle Jack was shot

And that my parents would be back home sometime soon
That would take days

My mother never really recovered from losing her brother
She spoke about him every day until the end of her life
I wanted to make her happy I wanted to ease her pain
Because I knew she was sad and I knew she was sick
I thought if I excelled and made something of myself like her
    brother did
She would be happy
And so I got to work

I started as an intern in a TV newsroom and worked my way up
I covered it all
I was hired, fired, and rehired
Overlooked, underestimated, and applauded
I won awards that I thought would make me feel successful
And they did for a moment, until they didn't

I raised four kids, buried both parents, and survived a marriage in
    the public eye
I've survived chaos betrayal and public humiliation
I protected my kids and showed up for them every day I could
I leaned on friends and family who guided me forward
And I rebuilt my career and worked my way back up in my
    own way

My main struggle has been for love
Letting it in
I'm working to break down the walls I have built
That keep it out

I've never wanted anyone else's life
I've wanted my own

I've wanted to understand why I'm here
And what I need to know so I can share it

And so at long last I know:

I'm not here to run for office or be compared to ghosts
I'm not here to walk the miles hoping you'll deem me enough
I'm not here to rest on my belly and not give a damn
I'm here to allow love in and let it out

I know I have the soul of a seeker
The heart of a warrior
The mind of a thinker
The drive of a visionary
And the spirit of a wild horse

I know I'm an artist a monastic a contemplative an introvert and
    an extrovert
I'm tough and I'm tender
Strong and frail
Feminine and masculine
Soft and gentle
Wise and curious
Restless and relentless
An agitator and an instigator

Yes, all those things can go together
I'm living proof and, probably, so are you

I know I'm a lot, or so I've been told
But I'm finally good with that

I am a force of nature
I am Maria

The Open Field

I hear you calling
Calling my soul
I long to go but somehow my feet will not move
They stand stuck where I am
But I can see where I need to go

I can close my eyes and see it
I smell the fresh grass
I feel the wind on my face
Finally the wind is soft
I no longer need it to batter me

I'm growing
Yes I'm growing
My feet are moving
One step closer to my soul's longing

I close my eyes
I can see the vastness
The breadth of space no longer scares me
I no longer need the fence to close me in
I'm growing
I'm growing

I hear that voice within me
You once were muffled behind torrents of tears
Now I hear you
Once so faint that I couldn't make out the words
Much less who they came from

But today I know that voice to be mine
I no longer sense the trembling

I'm growing
Let me speak
Let me speak
I'm growing

My feet now move
My voice now works
My heart still beats
My mind is becoming clear

I no longer fear the wind the rain the dark of night
I no longer fear that I don't know where the Open Field is
I no longer fear that I may stand alone
I'm growing
I've grown into me

The Open Field
Out beyond as Rumi said
Out beyond as the Almighty said
Out beyond
I'll meet you there
I'm here
I've grown
Look at me

EPILOGUE

And so, here we are. Everywhere I seem to look these days, I see people suffering from pain and heartbreak. Struggle and loneliness. I sense a yearning for something different, something more spiritual. What *is* often feels fragile and uncertain, and everything we thought we knew about ourselves and the world seems to change by the day. We are told these are unprecedented times, but I think this is simply life.

In this time of constant change and constant noise, each of us has an opportunity for introspection, an awakening, and a more fulfilling life. All of the old rules are gone, which means it's a good time for each and every one of us to dig deep and ask ourselves why am I here, what is my purpose, who do I want to become, how do I want to leave a mark on this world, and do I have the courage to examine and possibly alter old beliefs that may be keeping me stuck in a life I'm not meant to be in?

Life offers a full range of experiences and emotions to each of us. No one escapes the forces and events we are sure will break us.

But understanding that those same events are as much a part of one's life as achieving our dreams—getting that perfect job, falling in love, having a baby—is a valuable life lesson. Having a full, meaningful life means embracing the whole of life—the perceived bad as well as the perceived good.

That's the goal of my poetry: to embrace the whole of life. To awaken, to unearth, and to evolve and grow in a new direction. One's own.

My hope is that these poems spark a desire within you to write your own way to a deeper understanding of your childhood, your purpose, your life, and the lives of others. And my hope is that you don't wait as long as I did to be kind to yourself and others, to be tender with yourself and others, and to allow yourself to see yourself as worthy and enough.

I also hope you, too, will write poetry from the front lines of your own life, because I've learned this: Poetry doesn't belong only to the lofty and idolized figures of the past centuries or even to those English majors who study them! Poetry belongs to all of us. I believe there's poetry within all of us. It's an awe-generating craft. It's a healing tool—for each of us and the world.

AFTER FINISHING THE FIRST DRAFT of this manuscript in summer 2023, I traveled to Hyannisport, Massachusetts. This was the place where, for many years, I spent summers with my parents, my brothers, and my extended family.

My time in Hyannisport growing up was fun, but it was also highly volatile and very patriarchal. At times, it was actually quite dysfunctional, chaotic, and often felt unsafe.

Visiting Hyannisport used to trigger me. As soon as I'd land, I could feel my body tense up. I went on high alert. I was always ready to defend myself and to compete. Being there felt like survival of the fittest.

But something unexpected happened on my trip that summer. I felt a new feeling overcome me. I actually felt happy there. I felt present. I felt free. I had fun and enjoyed quality time with my family and extended family. I felt their love, their acceptance, and their joy. I felt seen for who I was. I felt at home.

I can't tell you how big this was for me. All the interior work I've done—all the excavating and peeling back of my layers— allowed me to stand there amidst my family, put my heart on the line, and feel unafraid that someone would trample over me. My trip home that summer allowed me to feel love and feel like I belonged. I felt safe. That was huge.

Now, just because I was able to finally have this moment doesn't mean my quest for myself is over. Nor does it mean that I'll never go back into the lion's den and feel triggered again. But it does mean that the old stories that kept me away for years have finally been buried. It means that the version of me that had my fists up all the time—ready to fight, ready to defend—no longer needs to live on guard.

I now feel like I can walk into this next chapter of my life with my heart leading me forward.

BEFORE I LEFT MASSACHUSETTS, I went to visit my parents, who are buried side by side. I sat and spoke to them individually and as a team. I know they both wish they could have been different at times. As did I.

For years, it was hard for me to understand them and their

choices. I spent a lot of time feeling unseen, unprotected, and alone while also still deeply loving them for being my parents. It was confusing to feel so many different things. Deep down, I think I was angry that I felt I had to suit up and be tough and "on" all the time. And yet, suiting up is exactly what helped me survive so many challenges in my life. It's also what led me to where I'm at now.

So today instead of being angry at my parents, I feel so much love for them, which makes me happy. My poetry has helped me unearth my childhood. I've taken off the sheath that I dragged with me all those decades. It may have gotten me here, but it didn't allow me to feel the love I craved, desired, and wanted.

Today, I also feel I understand my parents as human beings far better than I ever did before. I'm hopeful they understand me better as well. I hope they understand why I had to break away, and why I felt I needed to chart my own path. I'm sure that my choice to leave home caused them pain, particularly my mother. As a mother myself, I now look at those kinds of choices differently. While I don't regret the decision to move across the country, I do wish my parents and I had figured out a better way to spend one-on-one time together—time that was meant for just us and that didn't involve work or anything in the public eye.

So here I stand now in this moment, with my head back and my hair unruly. My laugh is deep, and my heart is expansive, vulnerable, shy, and tender. It feels so young. My life is full of new ventures and adventures, new loved ones and little ones. I feel alive, energized and at peace.

And yet, I know there's still so much life left in me. There are still so many parts of my story that remain to be written. Really truly.

In fact, just a few weeks before I turned in the final pages of this book, I had a wild vision come to me during one of my morning meditations: a vivid image of me giving birth to a new version of myself. It was a clear vision of a woman asking to be born and waiting to be unveiled. She said to me, "I'm another side of you that's been waiting for so long to come out. I'm a very feminine artist and I want you to tap into my creativity, my beauty, my tenderness, and my wholeness. The time is now to bring me to life. Here I am."

The vision made me weep. I wept for how hard I have driven myself. I wept because I could hear this other side of me inside saying, "It's okay. You're enough. Allow for this miracle to be born. It's you too. Give way and get out of the way of what's coming."

Shortly after this happened, I shared the experience in an essay in my weekly publication, The Sunday Paper. Thousands of readers wrote me to say they felt their own internal stirrings, but one woman's words in particular really moved me.

"Every detail of this story has profound meaning and clues to your own unveiling and discovery," she wrote. "What has been stolen from you or obliterated? What is sacred to you that's returning? Who or what is here trying to get your attention? What or where is home?"

These are profound questions that I believe we can all benefit from asking ourselves. I've been asking them of myself every day since.

Each and every one of us has a different version of ourselves deep within us that's ready to be born. For years, I didn't think this creative, artistic side of me could survive in this world, so I buried her deep within for the longest time. Now I've finally found the courage to let her come alive.

None of us knows what a new chapter in our lives will bring, but we can sense when an old one is over.

I stand in such a moment now. I no longer feel contained. I feel wild and free. I feel in communion with myself, with my God, and with others. I feel like I'm home.

ACKNOWLEDGMENTS

This book wouldn't have been possible if it weren't for the many people who've helped me rise, who've helped me rediscover my authentic being, who've helped me find my voice and carry on. I am deeply grateful to each of them for their love, their strength, their patience, and their rock-solid friendship.

At long last I finally and truly see myself as a writer, and that in large part has to do with my dear friend Roberta Hollander. I met Roberta decades ago when I went to work at CBS News. She was a legendary producer, and I was a green reporter who in her eyes was also a terrible writer. Every script I turned in to her was sent back marked up in red with comments about my grammar and my writing. I stayed at it, and over the years, the red lines became fewer, and slowly I got a compliment or two from her—which was, as anyone who worked with her knows, the highest praise I could receive.

Today I write all the time—columns, speeches, poems. It's something I've come to enjoy. It's something that has helped me not just to heal, but to also make sense of the world. I wouldn't be the writer I am today without Roberta's guidance, sharp eye, and fearless honesty. She is herself an extraordinary writer, editor, and thinker, and she makes every book I've written better. I tell her I love her all the time. I don't think she hears me. So I'm saying it here again: I love you, Roberta. I admire your journalism, and your honesty. I'm proud to have been your student. Thank you for your guidance throughout my life, and thank you for your help with this book.

I'm also deeply grateful to my long-time agents and good friends Jan Miller and Shannon Marven. They were the first two people to read my poetry, and they encouraged me not only to publish it, but to be proud of it as well.

And there are more:

To Brian Tart, the publisher of The Open Field and a legendary figure in publishing: Thank you for your notes, your observations, and your belief in me. It means the world to me to be able to partner with you and bring so many inspiring voices forward into the world.

To Patti Peterson, who works alongside me every day and who proofread every version of this book (and there were so many versions): Thank you.

To Lindsay Wilkes-Edrington, who helped me edit this book in its final stages and who has pushed me forward as a poet and writer: Thank you for your talent, your writing, your editing, your support, your keen eye, and your friendship. You make my words better and you helped me go so much deeper here. You made this book more honest and more revelatory. You also encouraged me to go for it when I wondered whether I had the courage to do so. It's an honor to work with you on my writing, and this book would not have been what it is today without you.

To Cydney Weiner, Jaclyn Levin, and the entire Shriver Media team: You are the best in the business (and I've worked with a lot of journalists over the years). Thank you for your excellence week in and week out. I'm so honored to work alongside you.

And finally, thank you to all the poets I have read and who have inspired me along the way. I'm grateful to write alongside you. Thank you in particular to my hero, poet Mary Oliver, whose poetry changed my life and who encouraged me to write poetry myself. Thank you for not laughing at me when I read some of my poems to you. Thank you instead for believing in me and pushing me forward on my own journey. I miss you and love you so. I'd also like to thank poet Emily Dickinson, whose voice continues to inspire me. Her famous line "I am out with lanterns, looking for myself" is one of my favorites. It perfectly sums up how I feel about my life's work and this book.

And to my children, my brothers and their families, and my circle of friends old and new: Thank you for helping me dig down and discover that I really was the treasure you told me I was. I love you with my whole heart, and I will love you until the end of God's time!

Xoxo,
Maria